THIS IS
INDONESIA

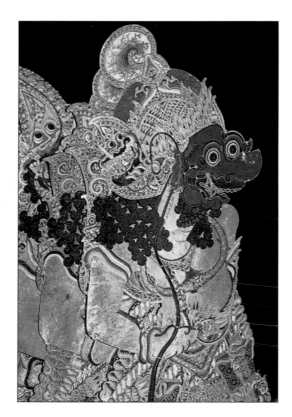

THIS IS
INDONESIA

Text by Christopher Scarlett
Photographs by Gerald Cubitt

NEW
HOLLAND

Photographic Acknowledgements

The publishers and photographers extend their thanks to the following people who kindly
loaned their photographs for inclusion in this book. All the photographs in the book,
with the exception of those listed below, were taken by Gerald Cubitt.

Wing Commander C.T.K. Cody: page 56 (below), page 75 (above), page 98 (above), page 102 (above),
page 122 (above and below left), page 125 (above right and above left),
page 140 (above), page 144 (below right)

Footprints: page 68 (above), page 69 (below), page 70 (below), page 73 (below right),
page 94 (above right), page 125 (below)

Jill Gocher: page 3, page 7, page 61 (above and below right), page 68 (below), page 94 (above left), page 95,
page 97 (below), page 99, page 102 (below left), page 111 (below right), page 115 (above),
page 119 (above and below left), page 123, page 128 (below left), page 129 (below),
page 130 (below), page 131 (below), page 133 (above and below right), page 135,
page 139 (above), page 141 (below left), page 142 (below left)

Indonesian Embassy: page 121 (above)

Caroline Jones: page 115 (below), page 129 (above)

Neil McAllister: page 1, page 61 (below left), page 69 (above), page 70 (above), page 111 (below left),
page 124 (below left and below right), page 128 (above), page 130 (above), page 133 (below left), page 138 (above),
page 140 (centre and below), page 142 (below right), page 143, page 144 (below left), page 145 (above left and below)

Tim Motion: page 4, page 5, page 6, page 11, page 100 (below), page 108 (above, below left and below right), page 111 (above)
page 124 (centre left), page 131 (above), page 134, page 138 (below), page 145 (centre)

Bob Pateman: page 98 (below), page 114 (above), page 119 (below right), page 120,
page 122 (below right), page 128 (below right), page 136 (below), page 141 (above), page 142 (above)

Linda Pitkin: page 146 (above right), page 148 (below), page 149,
page 150, page 151, page 152-3, page 153 (above), page 176

Royal Geographical Society: pages 12-49

Illustrations appearing in the preliminary pages are as follows:
HALF TITLE: *Wayang Kulit* shadow puppet, Java.
FRONTISPIECE: Rice paddies in Torajaland, Sulawesi.
TITLE PAGE: Bali dancers.
PAGE 4: Balcony with bird cages, Ambon.
PAGE 5: Detail of Toraja house, Sulawesi.
PAGE 7: Traditional performance of the *Baris* dance, Bali.
PAGE 10: Sunset from Ternate island, Maluku.
PAGE 11: Bali Outrigger, Sanur beach at dawn.
BELOW: Boat-painting in the old port of Jakarta, Sunda Kelapa.

ACKNOWLEDGEMENTS

The author, photographers and publishers would like
to express their gratitude to the following for their generous and valuable assistance during the preparation of this book:

INDONESIA
Joop Avē, Minister of Tourism
Andi Mappisammeng, Director-General of Tourism, Indonesia
Udin Saifuddin, Marketing Director, Directorate General of Tourism
Peter Pangaribuan and Zain Sumedy, Directorate General of Tourism
Mandarin Oriental, Jakarta • WWF Programme Office (Indonesia)
Drs Effendy Sumardja, Head of Forestry, Bali
The Central and Field staff of the Offices of Natural Resources and Nature Conservation
Garuda Indonesia • Merpati Nusantara Airlines • Indoavia Air Charter
Dr Kathy Mackinnon • Dr Charles Santiapillai
Drh Linus Simanjuntak, Ragunan Zoo, Jakarta
Dr Birutē Galdikas, Orangutan Research & Conservation Project, Tanjung Puting
Aristedes Katoppo and Aco Manafe, MUTIARA (Surat Kabar Mingguan)
Don Hasman • Robby Semeru • Des Alwi • J.B. Ridgeway
Jack Daniels, Spice Islands Cruises
Stanley Allison, P.T. Aerowisata
Drg Halim Indrakusuma sulia, Pacto Tours, and Heyder Souisa
David Heckman, Sobek Expeditions
Treesnawarty Madaning, Insatra Exclusive Tours, Sulawesi
Freeport Indonesia • Hotels Nusa Dua Beach and Sanur Beach, Bali
Senggigi Beach Hotel, Lombok • Heritage Sarana Resorts

SINGAPORE
Dr Peter Ng, National University of Singapore

GREAT BRITAIN
The Embassy of the Republic of Indonesia, London
The Indonesian Tourist Promotion Office, London
Pertamina Representative Office for London
Royal Botanic Gardens, Kew:
Dr John Dransfield • Dr Mark Cheek • Dr Philip Cribb
Royal Botanic Garden, Edinburgh:
Dr George Argent • Rosemary Smith • Maureen Warwick • Dr Roy Watling
Natural History Museum, London:
Dr Colin McCarthy • Dr Dick Vane-Wright

Special thanks also go to:
Ken Scriven • Janet Cubitt
Tony and Jane Whitten
D.D.F.E. Resources
The Royal Geographical Society

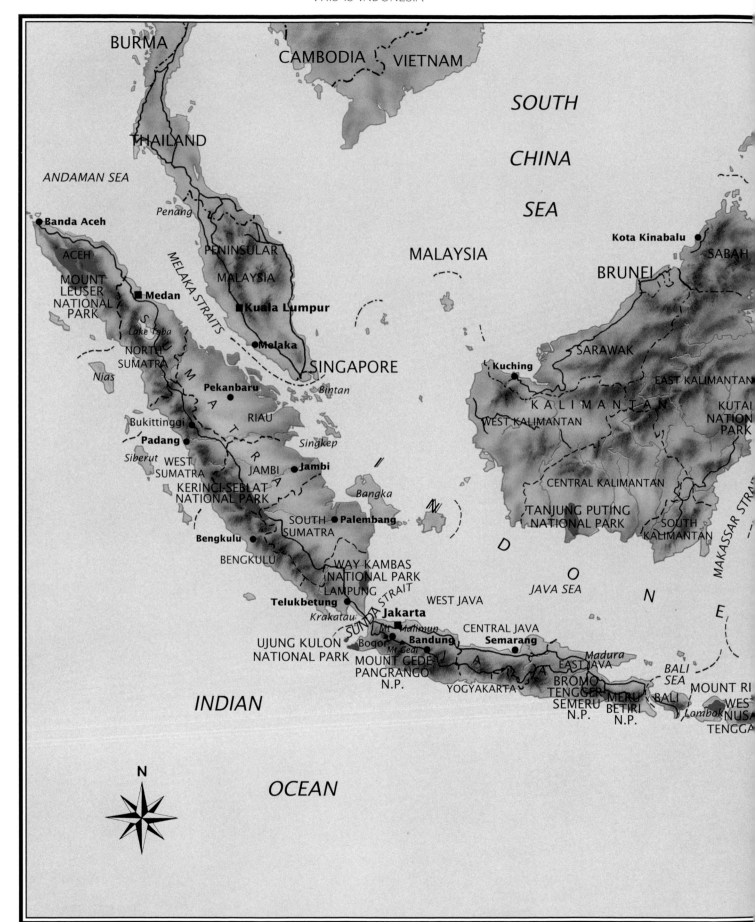

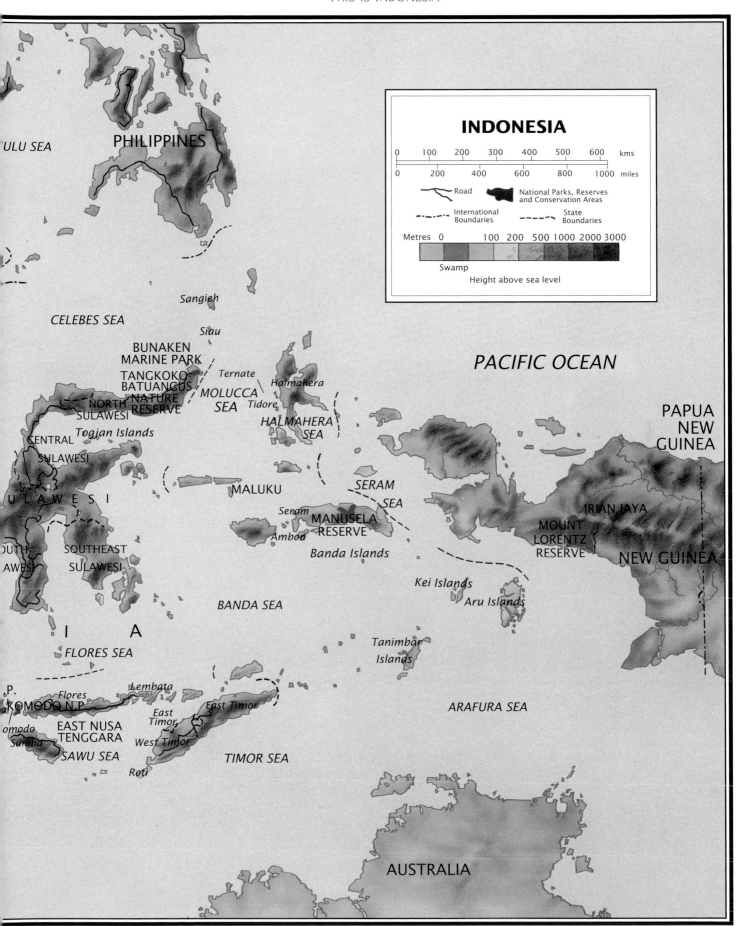

INDONESIA

| | 0 | 100 | 200 | 300 | 400 | 500 | 600 | kms |
| 0 | | 200 | 400 | | 600 | 800 | 1000 | miles |

Road — National Parks, Reserves and Conservation Areas

International Boundaries — State Boundaries

Metres 0 | 100 | 200 | 500 | 1000 | 2000 | 3000

Swamp

Height above sea level

PHILIPPINES

SULU SEA

CELEBES SEA

Sangieh

Siau

BUNAKEN MARINE PARK

TANGKOKO BATUANGUS NATURE RESERVE

Ternate

Halmahera

Tidore

MOLUCCA SEA

NORTH SULAWESI

CENTRAL SULAWESI

Togian Islands

HALMAHERA SEA

SULAWESI

MALUKU

SERAM SEA

Seram

MANUSELA RESERVE

Ambon

Banda Islands

SOUTHEAST SULAWESI

SOUTH AWESI

PACIFIC OCEAN

PAPUA NEW GUINEA

IRIAN JAYA

MOUNT LORENTZ RESERVE

NEW GUINEA

Kei Islands

Aru Islands

BANDA SEA

I A

FLORES SEA

Tanimbar Islands

P.

KOMODO N.P.

Flores

Lembata

East Timor

East Timor

ARAFURA SEA

omodo

Sumba

EAST NUSA TENGGARA

West Timor

SAWU SEA

Roti

TIMOR SEA

AUSTRALIA

PREFACE

Indonesia's people are many and varied. Separated, one race from another, by sometimes vast distances, they have developed a multiplicity of lifestyles and customs, absorbing during the course of their long and colourful history the influences of other lands. Yet, despite their differences, they are welded together by a strong sense of belonging to one nation. In their work, religions, customs and arts they celebrate in a thousand ways their pride and pleasure in being Indonesian.

The beautiful land that these peoples inhabit has, in turn, perhaps more divresity than anywhere else on earth — deep green rainforests, snow-capped mountains, rich valleys and an incredible range of animals, birds and plants. This wonderful natural heritage, and the cultural heritage that is so closely bound to it, cannot be isolated from the advances of the twenty-first century. The cities have become international gateways, industry thrives and the increase in tourism brings more visitors every year in search of new places and excitements.

Indonesia does not turn away from its future but is fully aware that its growth as a nation must be reconciled with the need to conserve all that makes Indonesia unique, be it the age-old values of traditional societies, the wildlife, or the spectacular landscapes. *This is Indonesia* is a portrait of all that is treasured in the country.

Christopher Scarlett
Chairman, Anglo-Indonesian Society
London

PROFILE OF INDONESIA

Indonesia lies like an inverted sickle along the equator, emerging from behind the Malay Peninsula and stretching east for 6,400 kilometres (3,980 miles) to the island of New Guinea off the north coast of Australia. Within this archipelago, the largest in the world, are estimated to be some 13,700 green and tropical islands, a mere fraction of them inhabited. Some, just tiny specks sprinkled in the vastness of the surrounding seas, are visible only at low tide. Although the total land area is around 2 million square kilometres (3/4 million square miles), this is dwarfed by the sea area, which is two and a half times greater. The Indonesians' description of their country, *Tanah Air Kita* – 'Our Land and Water' – is truly apt.

Dominating a spectacular variety of landscapes are volcanoes – many of them highly active – strung along the archipelago from end to end. Dense forests, packed with botanical riches and concealing fascinating rarities of the animal kingdom, appear to spread into infinity. Fertile plains, snow-capped mountains, sweltering mangroves – again and again the scene changes.

Equally diverse are the peoples of this unique country. Around 215 million inhabitants of complex ethnic origins, speaking hundreds of different languages and dialects, are proud to call themselves Indonesians.

Well over half this population lives in Java, which, together with Sumatra, Kalimantan (Indonesian Borneo) and other smaller islands, including the traveller's paradise of Bali, lies in Western Indonesia. Beyond these are Sulawesi, placed in the ocean like a strange scribble, the island groups of Maluku – the famed Spice Islands – and Nusa Tenggara, until finally, in the far east, the archipelago comes to an end with West Papua (Irian Jaya), the Indonesian half of New Guinea.

THE LAND

ORIGINS

The islands of Indonesia were formed by fire and violence. They lie at the meeting-point of four tectonic plates, which, shifting and colliding in the geological past, rose and folded along their margins, throwing up land above the oceans. Along these fracture lines a chain of peaks was thrust upwards by titanic eruptions. This intense volcanic activity still continues to disturb the area today.

The western islands are situated on an extension of the Eurasian landmass known as the Sunda Shelf. This is an area of shallow waters, not much more than 40 metres (130 feet) deep at most, which from time to time has dried out, as sea levels have fallen, providing land bridges between now separate islands. To the east is the Sahul Shelf, a stable extension of the Australian continent on the northern border of which lies New Guinea. Between the two stable shelves lies an area of recent tectonic activity comprising Sulawesi, Maluku and Nusa Tenggara. This is an area of deep water that has never been connected to either the Australian or the Eurasian landmasses and it is here that the four plates meet and four fracture lines radiate. The movement of two tectonic plates along the fault line to the West of Sumatra caused the disastrous tsunami of 26 December 2004 which, in North Sumatra alone, killed a confirmed 127,000 people, with a further 120,000 missing, presumed dead.

PREVIOUS PAGES

Page 12, above left: *Street scene in Batavia at the beginning of the last century. This former Dutch town has long been engulfed by high-rise Jakarta.*
Above right: *The great Hindu temple complex of Prambanan dates from the 9th century. Here, superbly carved stonework depicts figures from Hindu legends.*
Below left: *Bamboo house at Makassar (Ujung Pandang), Sulawesi, 1911. Light but strong, bamboo is still widely used as a construction material throughout Indonesia.*
Below right: *Small boats clutter the river at Palembang, Sumatra, 1900. Palembang has been a major port for well over a thousand years.*
Page 13: *Boats crossing the surf on Lombok Island, 1911.*

PREHISTORY

Primitive man arrived in Indonesia very early. Fossilized bones of the ape-like *Homo modjokertensis* and the slightly later *Pithecanthropus erectus* (the so-called 'Java Man') found in the Trinil area of Central Java date from the beginning of the Pleistocene era, something like 1.5 million years ago. These early Javanese are now accepted as being members of the near-human species *Homo erectus*, at this time widespread over Africa, Europe and China. Fossils indicate that these hominids used tools and had discovered the use of fire. Remains of a later and more advanced *Homo erectus* ('Solo Man'), dating from the end of the Pleistocene era, were also found near Trinil, at Ngandong, in the 1930s.

It is probable that the first human immigrants to Indonesia arrived more than 30,000 years ago, though the earliest fossils of modern humans (*Homo sapiens*) yet found on Java are estimated to be about 11,000 years old.

The ancestors of modern Indonesians are thought to have arrived between 2500 and 1500 BC in two migratory waves, though some scholars tend to favour the theory of a sporadic but continuous migration. These migrants emanated from the Yunnan area of South China where the upper waters of the great Asian rivers – the Brahmaputra, the Hwang He, the Irrawaddy, the Mekong, the Salween and the Yangtze – run close to each other. Remnants of their neolithic cultures have persisted almost unchanged in some isolated inland areas of Indonesia until very recently. It is only within the last few decades that modern communications have begun to change them (see page 29).

Before the end of this migratory period the Neolithic Age gave way to the Bronze Age in Indonesia. The major influence so far discovered was the Dong Son bronze culture emanating from Vietnam some time around the 7th century BC. This was characterized by a highly developed bronze-casting technique, some magnificent examples of which are seen in their socketed axes and ceremonial kettle drums, the largest of which was found at Pejeng on Bali, though it may not have originated from there.

By the Dong Son period Indonesian society was well organized and growing in sophistication. Traditional cultural life included music, puppetry and the practice of the fighting arts. The intricate form of weaving known as *ikat* was already being produced and traces of this ancient artistry are still discernible in the modern weaving of the Bataks, the Torajas and the Penan.

Embryonic towns were taking shape and a system of rice irrigation using bamboo pipes had been developed. The management and control of land led, in Java, to the formation of minor kingdoms by the 1st century AD. This control was codified into customary law, or *adat*, which persisted through subsequent religious invasions and, in fact, still persists today.

HISTORY AND GOVERNMENT

EARLY CIVILIZATION

By the beginning of the Christian era, Indonesia had developed a civilization of its own, primarily evident in Java and Sumatra. This was characterized by an agricultural society, based on the cultivation of rice, the domestication of the ox and buffalo, and a rudimentary use of metals. In spiritual matters, the cult of animism – the belief that all objects and natural phenomena possess living souls – predominated. Intermingled with this were strongly held beliefs in the deification of ancestors and a complex mythology of powerful supernatural beings.

Another characteristic of developing civilization was a skill in sea navigation. Early on in their history, Indonesians were making lengthy sea crossings to other lands and, in fact, they colonized Madagascar some centuries before the birth of Christ. These early sailors used Polynesian/Indonesian outrigger canoes, such as can still be found in the Indian Ocean in Sri Lanka, the Maldives, on the East African coast and on the west coast of Madagascar. It is unlikely that they made a direct crossing from Java to Madagascar, a distance of over 6,000 kilometres (3,700 miles). They probably sailed round the northern and western shores of the Indian Ocean and approached Madagascar from the west.

China was also a target for these intrepid voyagers. It is likely that Sumatrans had reached southern China by the beginning of the Christian era, although there is no evidence of direct sailings before the 3rd century AD. By then, China was already aware of Sumatra's importance on the trade route.

BUDDHIST AND HINDU INFLUENCES

The timing and manner of the arrival of Buddhist and Hindu teaching in Indonesia is complicated and uncertain. However, it is known that from the great centre of Buddhist sculpture at Amaravata on the River Kistna (Krishna) in central India, which flourished from AD 150-250, missionary Buddhist monks were sent to Indonesia to convert the courts and establish religious orders. This prompted a flow of pilgrims in the opposite direction. Many of these converts spent years away from their own country, bringing back to Indonesia the art and architecture of India.

The influence of Hinduism, unlike the missionary and proselytizing spirit of Buddhism, was exerted in a less direct way. It arrived from South India – the main contact point for trade with Indonesia in the early Christian era – where Brahminism, the teaching of the highest, or priestly, caste of the Hindus, was taking hold. It is unlikely that the traders themselves would have been interested in the scholarship and wisdom of a sacred cult. However, they did carry news of the developments brought about by the powerful Brahmins in the Indian royal courts. Inspired by such reports, the princes and nobles of Indonesia, who were at that time dominant in foreign trade, invited Brahmins to their own courts. They brought Indian concepts of royalty, the Sanskrit language, and epic poems such as the *Ramayana* and *Mahabharata*. They encouraged the observance of the 'laws of Manu', concerned only with the ruling classes and not the common people, which would have had immediate appeal.

In time, centres of both Buddhism and Hinduism evolved throughout Indonesia, for the most part with tolerance on either side. By the 7th century the first great Buddhist kingdom was arising in the area of what is

Bullock cart, Java, 1930. From earliest times, Indonesian civilization was based on an agricultural society. The domestication of the ox was one of its first characteristics.

now Palembang in south-east Sumatra. This was the kingdom of Srivijaya.

THE KINGDOMS

At the height of its power prior to AD 1000 the Srivijayan Empire controlled the whole of the Malay Peninsula, except the central highlands, as far north as Takuapa in what is now Thailand, the extreme west of Borneo and the western end of Java as well as its own territory in south-east Sumatra. Lying across the trade routes from China to the Middle East, this empire was to survive for six centuries on trade alone: it produced little itself except some timber products and even had to import rice.

Concurrent with the rise of the Srivijayan kingdom, and related to it, was the rich central Javanese kingdom of the Sailendra kings – the Lords of the Mountain. They too were Buddhists and it was they who erected the vast monument of Borobudur outside what is now Yogyakarta during the last decades of the 8th century. The Sailendra kings of Mataram and their Hindu vassal state ruled most of eastern Java at this time. Buddhism and the Sailendra kings lost power when the last adult member of the line, a woman, married the Hindu king of their vassal state. The ensuing Hindu revival produced the major temples on the Prambanan Plain between 898 and 928. The centre of power then shifted to East Java under King Sindok, who had the *Mahabharata* translated into Javanese.

As early as the 8th century, sea trade between the Near East and China was running into difficulties. In 758 Canton was burnt by an alien Muslim force and charges at the Chinese ports were becoming exorbitant. The collapse of the T'ang Dynasty and the cessation of seaborne trade between Persia and China all contributed to the decline of the Srivijayan Empire at the end of the 9th and beginning of the 10th centuries. By the time the Sung Dynasty restored some form of order, the isthmus trade had been taken over by the state of Tambralinga in southern Thailand. The Javanese state of Mataram launched a powerful naval attack on Palembang in 992 which was beaten off. Srivijaya retaliated in 1006 by attacking Mataram, burning the capital and destroying the ports and shipping.

Fresh misfortune arose when the Indian Tamil state of Chola attacked Srivijaya in 1025 and captured its king. However, Srivijaya's fortunes revived under a new king who formed an alliance in 1030 with King Airlangga of the erstwhile enemy kingdom in East Java. The dwindling Chinese trade was offset to a certain extent by the increasing importance of the spice trade and the Srivijayan Empire survived until the beginning of the 14th century.

King Airlangga died in 1049 and his empire was split, to be ruled by his sons as two separate states. Of these, Kediri became pre-eminent, profiting from the growing Mediterranean desire for spices. By the second half of the 13th century, Kediri,

from its new capital Singhasari, controlled eastern Java, Bali, parts of southern Borneo and Maluku, the key spice island of Ternate, the southern part of the Malay Peninsula and the Sunda Straits, and was contesting control of the Melaka Straits with a failing Srivijaya. Kediri also held Banka Island which lies across the mouth of Palembang harbour.

This brought hostile attention from Kublai Khan, the great Mongol emperor who had finally crushed the Southern Sung Dynasty and re-unified China by 1267. When Kertanagara, last of the Singhasari kings, refused a demand that he send a member of his family as hostage to the Chinese court, Kublai Khan launched two expeditions to the southern seas in 1292 to seek revenge. The first was an exploratory mission under the guise of escorting a Mongol princess to Persia. Marco Polo, returning from China to Europe, was a passenger on this expedition. The second landed on the eastern tip of Java in early 1293, where it heard that King Kertanagara had died and that the succession was in dispute. Vijaya, the legitimate heir, feigned acceptance of the Chinese demands and persuaded them to help him overthrow his rival. Returning with his captive, Vijaya turned on the Chinese troops and drove them back to their ships. The expedition sailed away having succeeded only in confirming the power of the dynasty it had been sent to overthrow.

Vijaya built a new capital at Majapahit and changed his name to Kertarajasa. In the interest of diplomatic relations, he married princesses from Bali, Borneo, Champa, on the east coast of Indo-China, and Malayu in southern Sumatra. His son succeeded him and was finally killed after numerous rebellions by a military aide at court, Gaja Mada, whose wife he had appropriated. The next ruler, Queen Tribhuvana, made Gaja Mada her chief minister in 1330 and he was to be the real ruler of Majapahit until his death in 1364. War with Sunda erupted viciously when the proposal that a Sunda princess should marry the next Majapahit ruler, Hayam Waruk, was pointedly rejected.

The Gaja Mada era of Majapahit was one of the most distinguished periods in Javanese history, when for the first time attempts were made to unite the whole of

Indonesia under one ruler. Majapahit power declined rapidly in the late 15th century when the establishment of Islam in the ports and coastal plains of Java forced the Majapahit rulers back into the interior. Many upper-class Javanese migrated to Bali and the final collapse of the Majapahit state occurred in about 1520.

THE COMING OF ISLAM

Until the mid-13th century the only established Muslim centres in Indonesia were at the northern tip of Sumatra, Perlak and later Pasai, Pedir and Aceh. Muslim Persian and Gujerati traders had long been resident in the coastal parts of East Java but they seem to have had very little interest in proselytizing among the local people.

The true rise of Islam in Indonesia was given impetus by the establishment of Melaka as one of the most powerful trading centres in South-east Asia. Founded at the end of the 14th century by Prince Parameswara, a descendant of the Srivijayan kings who had been driven out of his court at Palembang by Majapahit forces, the port was sited at the narrowest point of the Melaka Straits. At that time, the straits had been more or less closed to shipping for nearly a century because of pirate raids, curtailing vital commercial traffic. Re-opening the waterway was very much in the interests of the active Muslim trading centres of North Sumatra. It was also in the interests of the Chinese Ming Dynasty, whose prosperity was suffering from the closure by the Mongol war-lord, Tamerlane, of the Central Asian caravan routes from China to the Middle East.

In 1403, a Ming fleet charged with opening the straits to normal traffic called at Melaka and, as a result of this visit, Parameswara sent envoys to China in 1405. They returned the next year with a commission of appointment and a guarantee of recognition and protection. Protection was vital to the new state against hostilities from Siam and the Majapahit state that had exiled the king. He also received support from North Sumatra. In his old age Parameswara converted to Islam to strengthen his ties with the Muslims of Bengal and Gujerat who had long trading connections with the region. Subsequently many of the rich Arab, Bengali, Gujerati, Persian and Tamil merchants shifted their trading headquarters to Melaka from North Sumatra.

Melaka became the first Islamic mercantile centre in the region. Goods from the Middle Eastern ports of the Red Sea and the Persian Gulf joined the major cargoes of Indian cloth at the Gujerati assembly points whence they were shipped, mostly in Gujerati vessels, to Melaka. Here they were exchanged for spices brought from eastern Indonesia by the Javanese.

Trade emanating from Melaka carried the new religion and the commercial and political aspects of conversion were important in its acceptance. Those areas such as the Minangkabau highlands, the Batak highlands of North Sumatra and Bali, where there was little commercial and political incentive, opposed Islam vigorously. Java initially resisted the spread of Islam inland from the coastal Muslim city states, then repeated its reaction to the earlier pressures of Buddhism and Hinduism by absorbing the new ideas in so far as they fitted into ancient Javanese culture.

Melaka conquered Jambi and Palembang in the late 15th century, bringing them into the fold of Islam. Some fifty years later the middle portion of Sumatra's west coast also fell to Melaka. The Makassarese and the Bugis brought the new faith to Lombok and Sumbawa. By the 16th century the Muslim sultanates of Ternate and Tidore in Maluku held sway over an area from the shores of Irian Jaya in the east to parts of Mindanao in the north and to Bima in Sumbawa to the south. They also controlled Ambon, Banda, Buru, Ceram, and parts of Nusa Tenggara and Central Sulawesi.

THE COMING OF THE EUROPEANS
By the 16th century Indonesia was in a state of flux, with the Majapahit Empire in terminal decline, the Islamic trading ports on the north coast of Java spreading their influence inland and other Islamic states arising in Java, Sumatra, Maluku and South Sulawesi. Nevertheless, foreign and Indonesian ships sailed throughout the archipelago more or less freely, subject to the attention of the many pirates.

At the beginning of the century the Portuguese were embarking on an ambitious programme of exploration and expansion worldwide, coupled with a crusade against Islam. The highly profitable spice trade attracted them and they thought that this trade could be intercepted in the Melaka Straits: then, perhaps, the source of the trade could itself be tapped. Having captured Goa in southern India in 1510, they moved east and took Melaka the next year.

Although the Portuguese tried to fit in with the feudal trading patterns of Southeast Asia, they were not prepared to let ports such as Melaka remain as trading posts but wished to turn them into outposts of their European-based empire. Initially they attempted to encourage the normal trade of Melaka with the co-operation of the non-Muslim Indian traders and the Javanese. However, the rivalry for control of the spice monopoly soon became obvious and relations quickly degenerated. The Portuguese bid for control of the spice islands centred on Ternate and Tidore, whose sultans, although related by marriage, were bitter rivals. The smaller island, Ternate, had the better harbour and the Portuguese preferred to deal with its sultan rather than Tidore's. The eventual failure of the Portuguese to consolidate and maintain their presence in Indonesia was due largely to a lack of resources as a result of worldwide over-extension. In addition, their abuse of power and lack of interest in the local peoples meant that they were increasingly hated as rulers.

The Spanish arrived in South-east Asia under the command of a Portuguese, Ferdinand Magellan, as part of an ill-fated round-the-world expedition. They landed at Mactan in the Philippines, where Magellan and sixty of his men were killed. The last two ships of the expedition left Mactan and landed on Tidore on 8 November 1521. A later expedition established Spain's right to Tidore by agreement with the sultan.

The Portuguese attempted to reinforce their position in Maluku when they heard of the arrival of the Spanish, and intermittent warfare between the two powers and their various local allies continued. The Portuguese maintained a fort on Ternate until 1574 when they were driven out by the islanders who were enraged by the killing of their sultan by the colonial governor. They then moved down to Ambon where they established another fort, later returning to Tidore shortly before Sir Francis Drake's visit to Ternate in 1579.

The Dutch had been acting as middlemen, buying spices in the Portuguese ports and retailing them in northern Europe. But the Dutch War of Independence against the Spanish, together with the union of the Spanish and Portuguese crowns in 1580, effectively closed the Portuguese ports to them. They were forced to seek direct access to the sources of the spices. In 1595 a company was set up in Amsterdam to trade for spices in Indonesia; on 23 June of the next year four Dutch ships appeared in the Bay of Bantam. Although only three out of the four ships returned to Holland in 1597, the venture was considered successful enough to justify another, even more successful, expedition of eight vessels in 1598.

In 1602, to capitalize on their South-east Asian operations, Dutch traders formed their East India Company – the Vereenigde Oost-Indische Compagnie (VOC). Initially, they co-operated with the English East India Company as common allies against Spain, which was now also in control of Portugal. A factory was established by the two companies in Bantam, but the English had only a fraction of the resources of the Dutch and not much to offer except Indian cottons in exchange for spices. Relations became strained, leading to the eviction of the English from Bantam. All co-operation collapsed following the execution by the Dutch of two-thirds of the occupants of the English factory in Ambon. The English then moved their headquarters back to Bantam (where it remained from 1628 to 1682). In the meantime the Dutch governor-general, Jan Pieterzoon Coen, tired of the bad government and lawlessness of Bantam, took control of the VOC and in 1618 established a fortified trading post at Batavia, which was to be independent of Bantam. A major Javanese invasion from Mataram was defeated easily after its sea supply lines were cut by the Dutch, and Batavia continued to grow.

In 1621, Coen had also completely taken over the tiny spice-growing Banda Islands, and both these and Maluku suffered from the Dutch desire to curtail production of spices in order to keep the prices high. Surplus plants were destroyed when there was a threat of over-production and rebellious islanders were either eliminated entirely or sold as slaves in Java. By 1650 the Banda Islands were permitted to grow only cloves, and Ambon only nutmeg. Dutch power extended further into eastern Indonesia. Islamic Makassar in South Sulawesi held out for a long time as an independent free trade post but eventually fell in 1667. Melaka had already fallen in 1641 and now functioned as a place of exchange of cargoes and a military stronghold from which to control the straits. Trade moved to Batavia while Melaka continued to decline. The Dutch monopoly of the straits was weakened by their defeat at the hands of Cromwell in 1653-4, resulting in increased privileges for the English, and further by the joining of the Dutch and English crowns on the accession of William and Mary in 1689. However, the control of Indonesia remained firmly with the Dutch.

During the second half of the 17th century sugar was introduced into Java, where it was cultivated by the Chinese immigrants. However, pepper was the main item and Dutch pepper grown in West Java, Sumatra and Malaya was at one time supplying between 60 and 80 per cent of Europe's needs. Coffee was planted in Java in the first decade of the 18th century. Tea was brought by Chinese junks to Batavia, where it could be traded for not much more than the Canton cash price. It was then shipped to Europe in Dutch vessels. This trade continued even after the Dutch had been forced into the direct Canton tea trade by the English in the 1720s.

The establishment of British commercial control of South-east Asia from 1785 to 1825 emanated from India, where the English East India Company was assuming power. In Europe, Holland and France were at war with Britain in the early 1780s, and the Dutch renounced all claims to Southeast Asian monopoly in the subsequent Treaty of Rome of 1784. The threat of French interference forced the British to safeguard their way-stations at Cape of Good Hope, Mauritius and Ceylon. A way-station in the Melaka Straits at the island of

Bintan, off Singapore, had been proposed in 1769 by Francis Light of the English East India Company. Aceh and Kedah were also explored and Light was commissioned in 1786 to open negotiations with the sultan for a lease on the island of Penang. The British also acquired Melaka in 1795.

VOC competition was virtually eliminated when the Netherlands fell to French Republican forces in 1795. The state took over the assets and debts of the company in 1798-9 and, as successor to the stadtholder, sponsored a puppet Batavian Republic. The expelled Dutch stadtholder placed Dutch overseas possessions in British protective custody. The British were willing to allow the Batavian Republic to administer Java provided the French fleet was denied access. This arrangement continued until the European Batavian Republic was transformed into the Kingdom of Holland under Napoleon's brother Louis in 1806, effectively becoming part of France.

Louis Napoleon's governor, Marshal Herman Willem Daendals, arrived in Java in 1808 and proceeded to abandon most of the outer islands, except Makassar and Ambon, while he moved Batavia inland and fortified it against an expected attack by the British. The attack duly materialized and Java fell to the British in 1811 with the help

of Thomas Stamford Raffles, who was based in Melaka and had turned the native princes of Java against the concept of Franco-Dutch rule. Raffles became governor of Java.

In 1814 the Treaty of Paris put King William V on the throne of an independent Netherlands. The Dutch possessions in Indonesia, which had been held by the British during the annexation of the Batavian Republic, were to be returned to the Netherlands. Raffles acted slowly on this command and it was not until he was recalled to Calcutta in 1816 that the restitution was made. Although Raffles was governor for only about five years, he introduced a number of major reforms in the manner in which Java was administered and in its legal procedures. He attempted to discourage slavery and the import of opium, and declared an end to the system of compulsory deliveries of products to the State. This last was replaced by the *landrente*, or land rent, which remains in force today. Raffles was an enlightened and literate scholar as well as an administrator, and his scientific work over that period of five years is remarkable. His *History of Java*, published in 1817, is a formidable work.

The wars against the native Javanese waged by the Dutch in an attempt to reimpose their authority were time-consuming

Ambon, 1911. Ambon was one of the famed 'spice islands' of Maluku and scene of much bitter rivalry between European nations competing for a trade monopoly.

and very costly in terms of both men and money. It was decided that Indonesia should start to contribute to the state coffers rather than be a drain on them. Clearly this could be achieved only by force: the *kultuurstelsel* system was introduced by which Javanese landowners were obliged to make one fifth of their arable land available for the planting of crops as dictated by the colonial administration. They had then to plant and look after these crops until harvest, in return for which they were nominally (but often not in practice) released from the land tax and paid a very small sum for delivery of the harvested produce. This system could be imposed only where Dutch control was absolute and so, in fact, was largely confined to Java, with some outlying areas in Sumatra and Sulawesi also contributing.

Very large fortunes could be made by European and Indonesian entrepreneurs under these production contracts and naturally the abuses and corruption increased with the potential profits. At one point the *kultuurstelsel* was producing over 30 per cent of the total revenue of the Dutch government. Under pressure from liberal and free enterprise forces in Holland, the practice of *kultuurstelsel* was gradually phased out by the Sugar and Agrarian Law of 1870. The withdrawal of the government's monopoly greatly stimulated private capital investment in Indonesia and resulted in the growth of the great agricultural plantations.

During the second half of the 19th century the Dutch began a long series of local wars to bring the remainder of Indonesia under their control, until only Aceh in North Sumatra remained independent. By this time the opening of the Suez Canal meant that the Straits of Melaka were increasingly important and the inability of Aceh to control the pirates in the straits could no longer be tolerated. In 1871 Britain withdrew its long-standing guarantee of Acehnese independence and the Dutch moved against them in 1873. It was not until 1903 that the sultan and other chiefs finally surrendered and, even after that, sporadic rebellions and attacks continued until the Second World War, leaving Aceh economically broken.

The First World War had little impact on South-east Asia but led to a lot of discussion in Holland about future colonial ethics. Some form of emancipation of Indonesia was envisaged, though stopping short of independence. The possibility of an autonomous Indonesia with some kind of equality between Dutch and Indonesian residents was popular with many Dutch who had spent all their lives in the country and now wanted to spend their retirement there also. Some responsibility for having drained Indonesia for so many years was also felt and suggestions were made that the Dutch treasury should begin to contribute to the development of the country.

THE COMING OF INDEPENDENCE

Although the number of Indonesian students who had graduated from high school in 1940 was 240 (out of a population of 60 million) and the number who had studied in Europe was minuscule, the effect of the Dutch schools in Indonesia was more far-reaching that this would suggest. Even at the beginning of the 20th century, small but significant political student groups were forming, out of which sprang the first shoots of nationalism. However, Indonesian ideas of the way towards independence were confused by old provincial rivalries, differing views on modernization and a long-standing distrust of Javanese supremacy. The first important political party was the *Sarekat Islam*. This started as a trade association but became increasingly political and religious in nature. Eventually it was infiltrated by the communists who then went on to form the *Partai Komunis Indonesia* (PKI) while *Sarekat Islam* declined.

In 1927 the *Partai Nasionalis Indonesia* (PNI) was formed in Bandung under the chairmanship of Achmed Sukarno, who was eventually to become the first president of independent Indonesia. He was arrested in 1931 on charges on treason and served two years of a four-year detention sentence. In the meantime, two Sumatrans, Sutan Sjahrir and Mohammed Hatta, had returned from study in Holland and set up a separate, moderate socialist independence party which Sukarno merged with the PNI on his release. In 1934 he was again sent into detention, first in Flores and then in Bengkulu, and Hatta and Sjahrir were interned in Boven Digul prison camp on Irian Jaya.

The Japanese overran Indonesia in 1942 and initially looked to Muslim conservative opinion as easier to control and persuade to co-operate than the nationalist movement. Even before the war the Japanese Islamic Federation had been set up in Tokyo as an intelligence unit to formulate policy on Islam in Indonesia. After the invasion, Japan concentrated its attention on the Islamic Council of Indonesia (MIAI), which had been set up in Surabaya in 1937 as a federation of Islamic associations in Indonesia to challenge Dutch control of Islam. As the MIAI became more insistent on its demands – among others, for a Great Mosque and an Islamic university – the Japanese lost interest and it was disbanded in 1943.

On the political side, a puppet organization was set up to represent the Indonesian people under Japanese rule. PUTERA was formed, with Sukarno as chairman and with Hatta, Mansur and Dewantoro on its advisory council together with an equal number of Japanese. It had no popular support and was soon dissolved, to be followed, again under Sukarno and Hatta, by another organization, *Pusat Tenaga Rakyat*, designed to act on behalf of the Japanese in disseminating propaganda. By the end of 1944 military reverses had forced the Japanese to give a qualified promise of independence and to relax religious controls. In June 1945 a student conference issued the first call for full independence and on 14 August 1945 the Independence Preparatory Committee was formed, with Sukarno and Hatta at its head. Reluctant to declare independence, Sukarno and Hatta were kidnapped by a group of young nationalists and brought to Jakarta where, on 17 August 1945, the red and white flag of independent Indonesia was raised. Sukarno read the declaration: 'We, the people of Indonesia, hereby declare Indonesia's independence. Matters concerning the transfer of power and other matters will be executed in an orderly manner and in the shortest possible time.'

THE EVOLUTION OF THE MODERN STATE

Following the declaration of independence, the first cabinet of the new government of the Republic of Indonesia was formed on 5 September 1945. There were 16 ministers, with Sukarno as president and Mohammed Hatta as vice-president. The constitution was based on the *panca sila* or 'five principles': belief in the one and only God; just and civilized humanity; the unity of Indonesia; democracy guided by the inner wisdom in the unanimity arising out of deliberations amongst representatives; social justice for the whole of the people of Indonesia.

Anticipating the return of the Dutch, the fledgling government proceeded to organize itself politically and, in so far as it was able, militarily. When Australian and British forces landed in December 1945 to complete their dispersal of Japanese troops they found the new government already functioning in the main cities and in much of the countryside. It is to the credit of the British Command that the occupying troops confined their actions to consolidating their positions in the main towns and were not drawn into large-scale fighting with the Republican forces, in spite of many minor incidents and a more serious action in which a senior British officer was killed.

By this time the initial weakness of the political system had spawned numerous rival parties and a period of instability ensued during which the Dutch struggled to regain their former possessions. Holland signed two treaties with the Republicans in an attempt to come to a settlement, but on neither occasion was the outcome really acceptable to either country. With fears for his government's security in Jakarta, Sukarno transferred the capital to Yogyakarta in January 1946. In the following year the Dutch did indeed mount their first attack on Jakarta and other cities in Java and Sumatra.

In September 1948 communist factions launched a revolt in Madiun in which they attempted to exterminate all opposition groups in the area. Hatta assumed the presidency and he and Sukarno offered the people a choice between rule by the communists and a democratic regime headed by them. The armed forces overwhelmingly sided with Sukarno and Hatta and the uprising was put down. Using the resulting turmoil as cover, the Dutch launched a second attack, this time on Yogyakarta. Sukarno, Hatta and Sjahrir were captured and deported, first to Bangka and then to Prapat on the edge of Lake Toba in North Sumatra. An emergency Republican government was set up in Sumatra and a

guerrilla war started in Java and soon spread to Bali, Sulawesi and Kalimantan. This war was extremely costly in human life, particularly on the Indonesian side, but the Dutch were also finding the combination of the heavy human and financial losses and the mounting international pressure against them increasingly intolerable. Negotiations led in November 1949 to the transfer by the Dutch of sovereignty over the whole of Indonesia, except West Irian, to a Federal Republic of Indonesia.

Dissatisfaction with the federal system led to the creation of a unitary state under a new constitution in 1950. The early life of the Republic was marked by political chaos as parties formed, split, reformed and jockeyed for position. Revolts erupted in various parts of the country, the most serious of which was an attempt by the local contingents of the Royal Netherlands Indies Army in the island of Ambon to establish the Republic of South Maluku.

By 1957 political chaos had been joined by economic chaos following the end of the Korean War and the collapse of Indonesia's export commodity prices. Hatta resigned from the vice-presidency and, in February 1957, Sukarno proclaimed his 'guided democracy'. This was the start of what has been called 'almost ten years of the darkest and most irrational period in the Republic's history'. Sukarno was a great showman and a charismatic speaker, who for many years led the Indonesian people to believe in his impossible and unrealizable dreams. He embarked upon grandiose and expensive schemes such as the war against the Dutch for West Irian, which he won, and the *konfrontasi* against the British and Malaysia over the formation of Malaysia, which he disastrously lost. He tried to propel Indonesia to the front of the world stage by hosting the Asia-African conference in Bandung. He commissioned lavish projects such as the Merdeka Monument in Jakarta, a mosque designed to be the largest in the world and a vast sports stadium. The luxury of his lifestyle and his lack of contact with reality slowly eroded any form of democracy, as he assumed ever more grandiose titles for himself.

What Sukarno could not do was consolidate an economy already devastated by years of Japanese occupation and mismanagement. The government took over all

Dutch-owned companies and some 40,000 Dutch people left the country as a result. Huge increases in the prices of basic commodities and the removal of public sector subsidies were rapidly reflected in runaway inflation. Sukarno began to lean more and more heavily on communist aid and to endorse Chinese and Russian policies. The Communist Party of Indonesia (PKI), on whom Sukarno relied for power together with the army and his own Indonesian National Party (PNI), was estimated to be the largest communist party in the world by 1965. The PNI was also heavily infiltrated by the communists.

Tension between the army and the communists rose, culminating in a brief but unsuccessful communist coup in October 1965. A wave of anti-communism swept Indonesia which, combined with the settling of old scores and personal grudges, probably left somewhere in the region of half a million dead or imprisoned. After some months of this chaos, Sukarno was forced to sign the '11th of March order' which effectively placed governmental power in the hands of Suharto, who promptly banned the PKI. Sukarno remained president until the People's Consultative Assembly removed him from this position in March 1967 and elected Suharto as acting president. General elections were held in 1971 and Golkar, the party used to spearhead the army's political interests, not surprisingly won nearly two-thirds of the 360 elective seats in the Assembly; 207 non-elected members and 276 armed forces officers brought the total to 843. Suharto was then confirmed as president.

Indonesia immediately started to reverse its isolationist policies. It rejoined the United Nations, from which Sukarno had withdrawn, and joined with Malaysia, the Philippines, Singapore and Thailand in the formation of the Association of South East Asian Nations (ASEAN). The long, slow and undramatic process of rebuilding the economy was started with the setting up of BAPPENAS, the strategic economic planning unit staffed by western-trained technocrats to the extent that they became known as the 'Berkeley Mafia'.

Two major events occurred in the first years of the new order to damage the international reputation of Suharto's administration. The first was the financial collapse of the state oil and gas company, Pertamina, one of the largest corporations in the world. In 1973, it controlled the whole of Indonesia's oil production and had interests in everything from cement to real estate and telecommunications. This whole structure was built on an undocumented and unsustainable foundation of debt and mismanagement, and was practically free of government control. In 1973 the government tightened the regulations under which Pertamina could borrow money and by February 1975 the company was unable to meet its obligations. The government stepped in to guarantee its debts and the long process of tracing its liabilities began. Nearly two years later it was concluded that Pertamina's exposure ran to some US$10 billion.

Following this, the economy steadily strengthened until the Asian currency crisis of 1997, which led to the dramatic fall in value of the rupiah against the US dollar and left the country virtually bankrupt. Demonstrations in response to the economic crisis led to Suharto's resignation in 1998 and his replacement by Vice-President B. J. Habibie. Elections held in 1999 were won by the Indonesian Democratic Party for Struggle (PDI-P), headed by the daughter of former president Sukarno, Megawati Sukarnoputri. However, political tension on the streets of, principally, Jakarta, led the People's Consultative Assembly to reject Sukarnoputri in favour of the populist Abdurrahman Wahid, whose National Awakening Party (PKB) had come fourth in the elections. Wahid was forced to step down from the presidency in 2001, and was replaced by his vice-president, Megawati Sukarnoputri, with Hamzah Has, head of the United Development Party (PPP), which came third in the elections, as the new vice-president.

The second event to blight the early years of the Suharto administration was Indonesia's annexation of East Timor. In 1975 the eastern half of the island of Timor was occupied by the Portuguese, but was in the throes of a communist-led civil war of independence. Portugal chose to abandon its colony. In December 1975, in response to the small APODETI party which favoured incorporation of the territory into Indonesia, the Indonesian army invaded. In 1976, East Timor became the 27th province of Indonesia. Resentment at the incorporation festered and a guerilla movement flourished under the leadership of Xanana Gusmao.

Following Suharto's resignation, Habibie organized a referendum on 30 August 1999 to enable the East Timorese to decide whether to remain part of Indonesia. In spite of widespread intimidation, the vote was massively for independence. A caretaker government was established with the help of the United Nations, and a presidential election held in April 2002 was overwhelmingly won by Gusmao. East Timor became formally independent on 20 May 2002.

MODERN POLITICS

Elections are held every five years. Qualification of political parties is complex but the main political parties are the Indonesian Democratic Party of Struggle (PDI-P), which was formed out of the old Nationalist Party and a number of other secular and Christian parties; the Golkar Party (Golkar), a functional group that represents people such as civil servants, retired members of the Armed Forces, professional and womens' groups, students and farmers; the United Development Party (PPP), which was formed out of a fusion of a number of Muslim parties; the National Awakening Party (PKP), a moderate, mainstream Muslim party, and the National Mandate Party (PAN).

Traditionally, president and vice-president were appointed by the Peoples Consultative Assembly. However, from 2004 the president and vice-president are elected by universal suffrage of the (in 2004) 147.9 million electorate.

Qualifying political parties are elected by proportional representation within each province, which decides on delegates to send to the 550-member national House of Representatives (DPR). This broadly takes the place of the Peoples Consultative Assembly, as enshrined in the 1945 Constitution, but is entirely elected, with no appointees from, for example, the armed forces.

The Regional Representative Council (DPD) is composed of four individuals from each province, elected by proportional representation within that province.

At the provincial level, Regional Houses of Representatives are composed of members elected within each province by political party and, at district/municipal level, the Regional Houses of Representatives are elected in the same way.

The General Elections Commission (KPU) comprises 11 or less members at national level and is charged with the conduct of elections. There are provincial and district/municipal KPUs.

The Supreme Advisory Council is a body of 45 members, with a chairman and five vice-chairmen appointed by the president from among prominent public figures with a distinguished background in politics, administration or one of the functional groups. The Council responds to issues of national importance raised by the president for consideration or advice.

The function of the State Audit Board is to conduct official examinations of government financial accounts and to prepare detailed accounts of government revenue and expenditure. It also prepares a full report on the progress achieved in development and administration, which is appended to the President's annual speech to the House of Representatives.

The Supreme Court is the judicial arm of the State. It exists independently of the legislative and executive branches to exercise justice free from government intervention.

The day-to-day government of the country is in the hands of the president who appoints a cabinet. Each government department is under the overall control of a minister.

At the time of writing, the police and armed forces report directly to the President, but a bill is being discussed that is likely to change this, so that the police will soon report to the Minister of Home Affairs and the armed forces to the Minister of Defence.

MAJOR CITIES

Many of Indonesia's major cities are the legacy of centuries of trade which saw their development from small settlements to thriving international centres. Their past is strongly reflected in a mix of architectural styles from both east and west, and in the racial and cultural mix of their populations.

Jakarta, the capital, a vast sprawling metropolis of nine million people, encompasses the old town of Batavia where the Dutch built a fortress in the 17th century and grew rich on pepper, cloves and nutmeg. Surabaya, another of Java's historic trading ports, is still the point of departure for most

of the inter-island ships bound for eastern Indonesia. Yogyakarta is the cultural heart of Java, and some would say of the nation. Within the walls of the Sultan's palace, the Kraton, the traditional court arts continue to flourish and old rituals are preserved.

Medan, capital of the Province of North Sumatra, is very much a plantation city, owing its prosperity to the cultivation of tobacco. It contains many fine examples of colonial architecture and boasts one of the largest mosques in Indonesia. On the southern peninsula of Sulawesi, Ujung Pandang is an important port town of nearly one million inhabitants. Formerly known as Makassar, in the 17th century it was the gateway to the spice islands of Maluku. For centuries a great fleet of Bugis *praus* sailed out of Makassar to trade throughout the archipelago and beyond, and today they are sailing as proudly as ever. Jayapura, the capital of Irian Jaya, was established at the end of the 19th century. Then known as Hollandia, it was sited close to the border of German New Guinea to emphasise the Dutch claim to the western half of the island. Extremely hot and congested, the city has little of interest to the general visitor but it is the starting point for all expeditions into the interior.

INDONESIA'S NATURAL DIVERSITY

CLIMATE

Indonesia lies both north and south of the Equator but not far from it in either direction. The days vary little in length during the year and sunset and sunrise are at virtually the same time every day. Such seasons as there are consist of periods of hot and less hot, wet and less wet, though even these differences are minimal in West Java, Sumatra and Borneo. As you travel east the differences become more pronounced. Many islands in Nusa Tenggara are termed dry with an annual mean rainfall of less than 1,000 millimetres (40 inches) and there are pockets of very low rainfall such as Central Sulawesi with around 500 millimetres (20 inches). In parts of East Java the average rainfall is as little as 900 millimetres (35 inches) and droughts are known.

The rainfall is largely dependent on the direction of the monsoons. The westerly winds bring heavy rains from October to May, particularly on the western slopes of the highlands of Sumatra where average annual rainfall is 5,000–6,000 millimetres (200–240 inches); this compares with an annual average of 600–800 millimetres

(25–30 inches) in northern Europe. Maluku is affected by the north-east monsoon which gives it a wet season from April to July. Timor has a dry season which can last as long as seven months in the year and Irian Jaya, by contrast, has rainfall on the northern and southern slopes of the central highlands approaching the level of that of West Sumatra.

Indonesia, therefore, has plenty of water in its western islands; the problem is to stop it rushing off the land in flash floods, taking with it any loose topsoil. Irrigation is a matter more of control than of supply.

In addition to monsoonal rains, the country is subject to spectacular thunderstorms set off by unstable air masses rising over high ground or as a result of high surface temperatures. These storms can be extremely violent, with cumulo-nimbus clouds up to 15,000 metres (50,000 feet) and rain intensities of 300 millimetres (12 inches) per hour over a 15-minute period and a sustained record of 3,220 millimetres (130 inches) over 13 consecutive days. Very severe lightning and turbulence mean that the smaller regional aircraft could be torn apart by storms and even the largest jet will go to great trouble to avoid them. Another consequence of straddling the Equator is an absence of typhoons except, rarely and in mild form, in Timor.

Temperatures at sea level tend to be very high, around 30°–35°C (86°–95°F), and the humidity is high – perhaps 100 per cent at night in Sumatra and West Java. The highlands and mountain ranges, in contrast, can be very cold, especially at night. Temperature drops at a rate of about 2°C (3.6°F) per 300 metres (1,000 feet) of altitude so, when the temperature is 30°C (86°F) on the coast, it will drop to 15°C (59°F) even at a modest 2,000 metres (7,000 feet). This can feel cool and refreshing in the dry sunlight but distinctly chilly as the sun sets and the humidity goes up.

Indonesia's monsoonal climate brings drenching rains to much of the archipelago. This Paalaka tribesman of the 1920s had little to fear from the elements in his all-enveloping grass raincoat.

HABITATS

Indonesia's wonderfully rich mosaic of habitats is created by a combination of physical conditions, among the most important of which are climate and altitude. High temperatures and the humidity produced by the all-surrounding oceans sustain some of the richest vegetation in the world, but the islands are not uniformly clothed in tropical jungle. The eternal cycle of the monsoons and dramatic changes in altitude make for an astonishing variety of landscapes.

Much of the coastline is lined with mangrove swamps, where the trees are uniquely adapted to withstand the saline conditions and stifling atmosphere. Though little wildlife is evident here, the deep mud and murky waters around the tangled mangrove roots are inhabited by a strange and rich community of fish and amphibians. Behind the mangroves, peat swamps stretch inland towards the forests.

The great lowland rainforests of Sumatra, Kalimantan and Irian Jaya probably typify the kind of environment the visitor would expect to find in Indonesia. They contain an incredible diversity of plant species: fruit-bearing trees such as banana, tamarind and jackfruit, valuable timber-producing hard-woods such as teak and ebony, the aromatic Sandalwood and Kapur whose precious oils have been used for centuries. Many rainforest trees are immensely tall, their uppermost branches forming a dense spreading canopy, as much as 70 metres (230 feet) or more above the ground, that permits little sunlight to penetrate the lower levels.

A marked decrease in the height of the trees becomes apparent as the altitude increases. As the limit of the tropical rainforest is reached at about 1,000 metres (3,300 feet), smaller trees such as oaks and chestnuts appear and in the cooler atmosphere grow tree ferns and a number of other plants native to temperate climates. In the highlands, the trees become stunted and, as you go higher, give way to bushes shrouded in lichens which enjoy the humidity

caused by constant rainfall and perennial cloud and mist.

Above about 3,000 metres (10,000 feet) the vegetation becomes sparser still until, at the very tops of some of the mountains, it is too cold to support anything except moss and a little rough grass. At Indonesia's highest altitudes in Irian Jaya there is nothing but snow and ice. On the tallest peak of all, Puncak Jaya, 5,039

metres (16,532 feet) above sea level, flows one of the few glaciers in the tropics.

In the more seasonal areas of the archipelago, long periods of drought cause yet a further change in the landscape. Some of the drier regions to the east, such as Central Sulawesi, the south-east of Irian Jaya and Timor, are covered with savannah where few trees grow, though tall palms like the sugar-producing Lontar may rear their bushy crowns above the grass. Fires are a recurrent hazard here and most of the plants have evolved to be able to survive them. The fast-growing Eucalyptus is an example.

Man has profoundly altered much of Indonesia's natural environment. The fertile soils of the volcanic areas provide superb farming land and in islands such as Java intensive agriculture has replaced nearly 75 per cent of the original forest cover. In other parts of the country centuries of slash-and-burn agriculture have destroyed the primary rainforest but sustained cultivation has not taken its place, the result being a cover of scrub and comparatively low-growing jungle.

A Floral Heritage

There are over 30,000 flowering plant species in Indonesia's abundant flora, from the well-known begonias and Busy Lizzies to tropical exotica such as jacaranda, hibiscus and ginger. Some of the most striking are rhododendrons. They are found growing in large numbers in the montane forest, where the flaring colours of their flamboyant blooms splash across the scenery.

Thousands of orchid species have been discovered throughout the islands and many have still to be identified. They are usually epiphytic – that is, they grow on a host plant – though terrestrial species are also widespread. In bright or pastel hues, striped and spotted, intricately formed, they are one of the country's glories.

Fauna

During his travels in Indonesia in the middle of the 19th century, British zoologist Alfred Russel Wallace made the observation that the fauna to the east of Bali and Borneo were those associated with Australia, while those to the west of Lombok and Sulawesi were associated with the Indo-Malayan region of South-east Asia. It is now accepted that these divisions on either side of the so-called Wallace's Line are not as precise as was once thought. In fact, the groupings of certain animals are determined more by the biological influences of the Philippines, Maluku and Nusa Tenggara, and also in this area is found wildlife that is typical neither of the Australian nor the Malaysian sides.

The large mammals of western Indonesia

arrived from the north when the islands were covered with dense jungle. They remain only where lowland forest is still intact and the greatest threat to their existence, apart from poaching, is the clearing of forest for agriculture and intensive logging. The largest, the Asian Elephant, is found in Sumatra, and in Kalimantan, where it may have been introduced relatively recently. The biggest populations are concentrated in the Way Kambas National Park and the Air Sugihan Reserve in southern Sumatra where the lush vegetation can support fairly dense herds. Elephants love the succulent leaves of young bamboo, gingers and wild bananas; they also love oil palm, coconut and other cultivated crops. Being extremely destructive eaters, a herd can wipe out young plantations in very short order. Thus, although a protected species, they are a considerable nuisance which it is expensive to control by electric fences and other barriers. It seems likely that the fate of the elephant in Sumatra will be practical natural extinction in the not-too-distant future although it may perhaps survive in carefully controlled reserves.

The forests of Sumatra also support the increasingly rare two-horned Sumatran Rhinoceros which, like the elephant, is vulnerable through loss of its natural habitat and, even in the national parks, has been a target for hunters. Its larger cousin, the one-horned Javan Rhinoceros, found only in the Ujung Kulon National Park in West Java, is rarer still.

Of all the animals that visitors to Indonesia's parks most hope to see, the Sumatran Tiger probably heads the list. However, this beautiful elusive beast does not readily show itself. Its wide-ranging predatory habits mean that each animal needs a very large area, perhaps as much as 50 square kilometres (20 square miles), to maintain a reasonable level of survival.

The Orang-utan, found only in the jungles of Sumatra and Borneo, is one of the most impressive and famous apes in the world. A fully grown male is as large as a man and weighs as much. It moves around the forest at canopy height, swinging from tree to tree and using its own weight to bend branches where the gap is too great. It is a solitary beast, ranging over considerable areas and eating fruit and almost any-

thing else it can get its hands on. It makes a platform of woven branches high in a tree to sleep on every night and never uses the same one twice.

Orang-utans have been victims of an unfortunately profitable trade in the sale of their young as exotic pets. Such captives are now confiscated by the government to be reintroduced into the wild at rehabilitation centres such as the one in the Tanjung Puting National Park on the south coast of Kalimantan and the Bohorok Rehabilitation Station in the Gunung Leuser National Park, only a couple of hours' drive from the city of Medan in North Sumatra.

Among Indonesia's smaller primates are various species of gibbon, which are the most closely related primates to man, the Proboscis Monkey with its extraordinary long nose, the leaf monkeys which can often be seen swinging in large groups from tree to tree, and the numerous species of macaques, some of which are trained to harvest coconuts. The smallest are the nocturnal tarsiers: the Spectral Tarsier is a tiny creature with a body only 10 centimetres (4 inches) long and weighing less than 100 grams ($3^{1}/_{2}$ ounces) but with a tail twice as long as its body.

The world's smallest bear, the Sun Bear, is a native of the forests of Borneo and Sumatra where it is feared in spite of its small size. Being very short-sighted, it is easily surprised and will turn on an intruder with vicious claws. Wild pig are found all over Indonesia; the Warty Pig is hunted for sport in Java where it is common in teak plantations and secondary vegetation. The Babirusa of Sulawesi looks like a wild boar but is no relation and has tusks growing through its cheeks: a peculiarity unknown in any other animal. Bats of all types are common throughout the country with 90 species in Kalimantan alone. They vary from large Flying Foxes and fruit bats to tiny insect-eating bats living in holes in the stems of bamboo. The limestone caves of the region are favourite haunts of bats and clouds of tens of thousands emerge at dusk and return at dawn.

In Irian Jaya, though there are major areas of dense forest and swamp not unlike those of Sumatra and Kalimantan, the large mammals of Asia, such as the tiger, rhinoceros and elephant, are absent. Instead, a whole range of Australian-derived species occurs. These include wallabies, carnivorous mice (thought to be related to the extinct Tasmanian Wolf), bandicoots, flying possums like the Sugar Glider which uses the membrane stretched between its legs to glide from tree to tree, tree-kangaroos, which are quite at home in the branches but find walking difficult, and the Spiny Anteater, related to the Duck-billed Platypus, which lays a single egg and then carries the hatched young around in a marsupial pouch.

Most of Indonesia's many species of snake are harmless and all are shy with the exception of the Death Adder of Irian Jaya and Maluku, which is both aggressive and very poisonous. The sea snakes are all poisonous and the cobras and tiny kraits deadly. Crocodiles are now found mostly in Irian Jaya and, more rarely, in Kalimantan. The demand for their skins for handbags and shoes has led to extensive hunting and to the setting up of crocodile farms.

Indonesia is home to no less than 17 per cent of the world's known bird species. Sumatra and Kalimantan have some 450 species of which most are common to both islands and inhabit the lowland forests. The hornbills have been woven into the culture and decorative arts of the Dayak tribes of interior Kalimantan and the Rhinoceros Hornbill in particular is the dominant image of the area. The horny casque of the Helmeted Hornbill is hard and dense and is used for a wide range of carved decorative objects.

In Java and Bali there are over 300 species of birds but the high degree of both agricultural and urban development has caused some to be more common in captivity than in the wild. The Javanese particularly are great caged bird fanciers and rare examples command high prices. In any town or village in Java in the morning long bamboo poles can be seen outside the houses, each with a bird in a cage hoisted on its top to encourage it to sing.

In Maluku signs start to appear of the influence of Australian birds, most noticeably the parrots and cockatoos. Irian Jaya, as always, is a law unto itself with the hornbills and shrikes of Asia at their most easterly limit and a host of birds of Australian origin. There are over 40 species of parrot and over 20 species of birds of paradise. Only a few of the latter have the gorgeous plumage which

has made them so hunted for decoration both by the natives of Irian Jaya and for export over the centuries to other parts of South-east Asia and as far as Europe. Relatives of the birds of paradise are the bowerbirds which build intricate woven edifices with which to attract a mate. The male Bird's Head Bowerbird constructs a cone-shaped bower over a metre (3 feet) in height and diameter complete with a door and a front terrace which it decorates with flowers and fruit.

NATIONAL PARKS

The speed at which certain natural habitats are being disturbed or lost altogether, and the consequent threat to the survival of a wide range of plants and animals, has led to the establishment of a number of protected areas throughout Indonesia. Some are designed to safeguard a particular species, others to regenerate endangered species and to attempt to maintain an untouched environment in which the natural ecology may continue to thrive. Among the numerous areas, all of which contain much of interest, the following are perhaps among the most outstanding.

Mount Leuser National Park

Mount Leuser, in North Sumatra, is one of the largest forested areas in South-east Asia, covering nearly 95,000 square kilometres (3,670 square miles). Its habitats range from coastal forest to the soaring peaks of the Central Range, where Mount Leuser itself rears up to 3,381 metres (11,092 feet). The Alas River, turbulent after heavy rainfall, runs through the park, offering tourists the excitement of white-water rafting. The wildlife is rich and varied.

Mount Gede-Pangrango National Park

Surrounding the twin volcanoes of Mount Gede and Mount Pangrango, this 150 square kilometre (60 square mile) area is easily reached from Jakarta, capital city of Java. Well known for the conservation work that has been carried out within its confines, the park attracts visitors in search of its outstanding variety of animal and plant species.

Ujung Kulon National Park

Ujung Kulon is famous as one of the last refuges of the endangered Javan

Rhinoceros – although the chances of sighting this rare beast are extremely small. Sited on the westernmost tip of Java, the park covers 786 square kilometres (303 square miles) and has good examples of lowland forest, open grassland full of deer and wild cattle, mangrove swamps and unspoiled beaches.

Bromo-Tengger-Semeru National Park

The Bromo-Tengger-Semeru National Park in East Java is one of the great volcanic regions of Indonesia. The caldera of Mount Tengger, fully 10 kilometres (6 miles) across and containing the Bromo Crater, is a popular destination for tourists, who make the early morning trek to watch the sun rise over the crater walls. Surrounding Bromo is the famous Sea of Sand, a great stretch of sand and ash that swirls with mist in the morning light.

Tanjung Puting National Park

Tanjung Puting National Park, on the south coast of Kalimantan, comprises a 3,050 square kilometre (1,178 square mile) area of peat swamp and heath forest. The swamp, in the centre of the park, is interesting for wetland birds and crocodiles.

Orang-utans can be seen at the Camp Leakey Research Station and several other primates can be found, including the extraordinary Proboscis Monkey which frequents the coastal and riverine forests.

Manusela National Park

The major conservation area in Maluku, Manusela is a swathe of lowland and montane forest running from north to south across the centre of Seram, one of the largest islands in the province. The 1,890 square kilometres (730 square miles) of the park are exceptionally rich in endemic plant and animal species, and special areas have been reserved for the protection of birds, including the enormous flightless Cassowary.

Mount Rinjani National Park

The impressive peak of Mount Rinjani towers to 3,726 metres (12,224 feet) above the small island of Lombok, westernmost island in Nusa Tenggara. The mountain forms the centre of a national park, extending over 400 square kilometres (155 square miles), which is itself surrounded by a further area of protected land. At the bottom of Rinjani's huge crater lies the bright emerald Segara Anak lake, which pours out in a magnificent waterfall on the north-east side. Though a public road now runs to the lake, climbers and walkers have long found an irresistible thrill in hazarding the steep footpaths to the water's edge.

Bunaken Marine Park

Bunaken Island, lying just offshore from North Sulawesi's capital of Manado, is justly famous for its beautiful coral reefs which attract divers from all over the world. The shallow waters around the reefs team with brilliantly hued fish; delicate feathery sea fans extend in the currents while colourful communities of sponges, starfish, sea anemones and other marine life abound. On the sandy beaches, turtles come ashore to breed.

Bogani Nani Wartabone National Park

This park is the largest conservation area in Sulawesi, sprawling for about 3,000 square kilometres (1,160 square miles) in the long northern peninsula. The land, which rises from just above sea level to nearly 2,000 metres (6,600 feet) is characterized by dramatic limestone ridges and dense lowland rainforest. The two main rivers, the Dumoga and the Bone, are lined with eucalyptus trees. The Babirusa, whose numbers have unfortunately been reduced by hunting in the eastern half of the park, may still be found on the west side.

Komodo National Park

Between Sumbawa and Flores in Nusa Tenggara lies Komodo Island, renowned as the home of the world's heaviest lizard – the Komodo Dragon. The national park, with a total area of 750 square kilometres (290 square miles), in fact covers not just Komodo but three other small islands – Padar, Rinca and Gili Motang – as well as part of the mainland of Flores and some of the surrounding seas.

Komodo is mostly dry and hilly, though there is some lowland forest cover. The main reason for a visit is to see the huge carnivorous lizards in their natural state. These monsters can reach 2.8 metres (9 feet) in length and attain a weight of up to 50 kilo-

grams (110 pounds). They prey on deer, buffalo and other smaller animals and, although it is rare for them to attack humans, they can move quite fast and a close approach is not recommended. However, supervised trips to safe observation points can be arranged.

Mount Lorenz Reserve

The largest conservation area in Indonesia, the spectacular Mount Lorenz Reserve in central Irian Jaya covers around 21,500 square kilometres (8,300 square miles). High rugged limestone mountains, glaciers and snowfields, dense forest, plains and mangrove swamps are just some of its incredible range of habitats.

THE PEOPLES OF INDONESIA

ONE NATION, MANY PEOPLES

The peoples of Indonesia form a great pot-pourri of races, among whom striking differences are immediately evident. The sheer complexities of evolution – the gradual infiltration of the archipelago, far back in time, by peoples from all over mainland Asia, together with later influences from Arabia and Europe, shifts in population and intermarriage between tribes – have all but confounded attempts to trace clear-cut lines of origin for any one ethnic group. It would be impossible to give an account here of all of Indonesia's historic peoples, but certain major groups can be identified.

The Malays, now found throughout western Indonesia, originally occupied only the coast of the Melaka Straits and Kalimantan. They are believed to be the result of an extensive intermingling of Mongoloid-type peoples living around the ancient coastal trading routes. They are typically of slight build with broad faces, and a skin colour ranging from olive to reddish-brown; a Mongolian fold of the eyes is not uncommon. Malays are almost invariably Muslim.

In Sumatra, two of the largest ethnic groups are the Minangkabau and the Bataks. Pushed back into the interior by later arrivals, both have developed distinct characteristics in almost complete isolation from the peoples of the coast. The Minangkabau are Muslim, although they have kept their matrilineal customs. The

Bataks are now divided between Christianity and Islam, though many earlier animist customs and beliefs persist.

The Javanese are a fairly homogenous people belonging to the Oceanic or southern branch of the Mongoloid race. They are of slight build, small stature and often exquisite facial bone structure, with light golden-brown skins and straight black hair. The modern Balinese are largely immigrants from Java who have mixed to some extent with the original Balinese, the Bali Aga, now found only in a few walled villages in the interior.

In Kalimantan the non-Islamic peoples of the interior are known collectively as Dayaks, although they do not use the term themselves and it covers considerable cultural and language differences between the tribes. The Iban are the largest of these inland farming groups. They were formerly known as 'Sea Dayaks' because they were once coastal dwellers until pushed into the interior by the trading Malays and Bugis who came to settle on the coasts of Borneo.

The Penan or Punan were Borneo's earliest inhabitants. A number of tribes remain in the interior, still following their traditional nomadic existence as hunter-gatherers and living in communities of only a few dozen individuals. Their survival depends mainly on the products of the hill sago palm and on what they can glean from the jungle. They are expert with the blowpipe and use poisoned arrows to hunt wild pig.

Sulawesi contains six quite separate peoples: the Toala, the Toraja, the Buginese, the Makassarese, the Minahasan and the Gorontalese. The Toala are probably the true aboriginals of Sulawesi. They are short and dark with wavy or curly hair, a broad, flat nose and a prominent mouth. They are partly nomadic jungle dwellers but in the past groups were enslaved by the Buginese and other more disciplined tribes and now communities of Toala are found living within other tribal lands.

The Toraja are a collection of tribes living in isolated groups in sparsely populated parts of central, east and south-east Sulawesi. They have mingled with the Toala over the centuries and have been dominated by the Buginese and Makassarese, with the result that their previous animism is giving way to Christianity and Islam though, as so often in Indonesia, the old ways are very

much in evidence. They were once head-hunters living in fortified villages but now live in settled, open villages surrounded by gardens and orchards.

The Buginese, who live on the south-western peninsula of Sulawesi, and the Makassarese, who live on its southern tip, are probably descended from the Toraja. With the exception of language they have a great deal in common. Much of their culture is similar and they have been, and are, great shipbuilders and sailors. They have also been notorious pirates. Their outrigger *praus* are famous throughout the archipel-ago and early on they travelled as far as Australia in the south and Timor in the east. This contact with other peoples brought them under the influence of Islam and most

Bugis are now staunchly Muslim. The Makassarese retain rather more of their pre-Islamic beliefs and customs.

Between the Minahasan peoples of the extreme north-east of Sulawesi and the Toraja of the centre are the Gorontalese. They are related to the Toraja but not to the Minahasans, who are distinct from all the other peoples of Sulawesi. The Minahasans are related to the people of the islands of Siau and Sangieh which lie to the north. They are very light-skinned, tall and strong, with high noses, widely separated eyes and prominent lips. It is likely that they are a partly Caucasian immigrant race who arrived via the Philippines. The long occupation by the Dutch and the thorough Christianization of Manado, which was

A Bugis settlement at Balikpapan, in East Kalimantan, 1906.

readily accepted by the Manadonese, resulted in a large Eurasian population.

In the islands of eastern Indonesia the picture becomes even more complicated. Here the inhabitants evolved from an inter-mingling of Austronesian peoples from the west and Papuans from Melanesia in the east, the resulting ethnic groups varying from region to region. Subsequent invasions of people from Java and the west created a further ethnic mix in the smaller islands and along coastlines, while in the larger islands the earlier groups, such as the Atoni of Timor, were pushed further into the interior.

In addition, the peoples of Maluku show the effects of the long Portuguese and Dutch presence, particularly in Ambon: here there was a large Christian Eurasian population, many of whom emigrated to Holland after independence.

The island of New Guinea, the western half of which forms the Indonesian province of Irian Jaya, is the core of the Melanesian culture which stretches from Timor in the west to Fiji and New Caledonia in the east. Its people are Papuan, related to the peoples of the South Pacific, with very dark skins, round heads and woolly hair. The men are bearded and show a similarity to the aboriginals of Australia. The extremely high and difficult terrain of the interior of New Guinea, where each valley is isolated from its neighbour, has allowed different cultures to develop in close proximity but without contact with one another or the outside world over a very long period of time.

Lastly, the presence all over Indonesia of the Chinese must be noted. They are mostly from the southern Chinese provinces of Fukien and Guangdong and originally arrived as traders, settling on the coasts of Java and Sumatra astride the trade routes many centuries ago. Later arrivals have permeated the Indonesian economy to great effect and much of the personal wealth of Indonesia is today in the hands of the 3 per cent of the population which is of Chinese origin. The Chinese are also important in West Kalimantan as farmers and fishermen and in the Riau Archipelago as miners.

LANGUAGE

The variety of languages spoken in Indonesia is so great that a precise number is difficult to establish. By a conservative estimate, there are around 300 separate languages, each with a range of regional dialects that can be distinguished by differences in speech patterns and word forms within even comparatively small areas. This multitude of tongues can be related to two major linguistic families – the Austronesian group, which applies to almost all of Indonesia, and the Papuan group, the influences of which are heard largely in parts of Halmahera, in Maluku and in the highlands of Irian Jaya.

Serving as a common means of communication for all, the national language, Bahasa Indonesia, is widely known as a second language throughout the population. It is the only one used by the media and in official publications, and is taught from the earliest levels in schools. The basis of Bahasa Indonesia is Malay, though it contains many words borrowed from Sanskrit, Arabic, Portuguese, Dutch and English, reflecting the succession of cultures that permeated the archipelago down the centuries.

TRADITIONAL SOCIETIES

The organization of traditional society in Indonesia is, in large part, centred on the use people make of their land. Nowhere is this seen more strikingly than in Java and Bali, where the pressure of population combined with extremely rich soil has produced intensive wet rice cultivation. Since early times co-operative effort has been needed to control and share the water supply for irrigation and this has led to a formal system of mutual help and policing which survives as *adat* (customary law) to this day.

In Bali, as in Java, the basic unit is the village or *desa*, which consists of two streets at right angles lined with the family compounds: the Balinese like to have a wall around them. The square where the two streets intersect is the heart of the village where all the important communal events take place. It is the site of the marketplace, the village temple and the cockfighting arena and often also the giant banyan tree, sacred to the Hindu gods. Public baths, the cemetery and the temple of the dead will be on the outskirts of the village.

Within the community small co-operative groups of families known as *banjar* provide a basic self-help nucleus for ceremonies and the celebrations connected with birth, marriage and, especially, cremation. The *banjar* owns the community's *gamelan* and its dance properties. There is a *banjar* temple and a *banjar* house (the *bale banjar*) where members meet as in a club to discuss local affairs.

A further community association, the *subak*, has developed to administer the irrigation of the rice fields. All owners of land looking to a single source for water are members of the association and their collective responsibility is to control the distribution of water and to ensure that every owner, large or small, receives sufficient for his needs. An old saying recommends that the man whose fields are at the bottom of the hill be put in charge of the water. Members of the *subak* contribute fees to finance the maintenance of the irrigation system and to ensure that the correct offerings are made at the two *subak* temples, one at the water source and one among the fields. These fees were traditionally paid in work on communal projects but may also be paid in money or kind.

However and wherever it is grown, the harvested rice must be stored safely and Indonesia has evolved a range of traditional rice barns, often highly decorated. They consist of a chamber raised some distance off the ground and often have great upswept roofs like the horns of a buffalo. Rice barns are holy places where the rice spirit lives until it is time for the next crop and all communities have strict rules about who may enter them to take out supplies for the family. The design of the rice barn may denote its owner's rank, as do the three types of barn built on Lombok. In Tanatoraja in Sulawesi the space below the rice barn is the main social gathering-place of the village where people stop to gossip or discuss village affairs. It is also the place where marriages are arranged and disputes settled. A person's house is private; the rice barn is where public and private meet.

Outside Java and Bali, the pressure on land is less and, except in Sumatra, most rice grown is of the dry, upland variety. This is much less productive per square metre but requires little social organization. The basic unit of society therefore remains the family or extended family. The Dayaks of Kalimantan traditionally live in longhouses, erected beside a river and raised on stilts above the ground to provide shelter for live-stock and a measure of security against attack. Under their pitched roofs, longhouses are one room deep with each family having its own separate quarters but sharing a wide communal verandah running along the front of the house. They were once home to large numbers of families but have tended to become smaller in recent times. The Dayaks farm by the 'slash-and-burn' technique, clearing an area of forest and growing upland rice and vegetables until the soil is exhausted, when another area will be cleared while the previous one is left to regenerate.

The people of Tanatoraja continue to observe a very strict *adat* related to the three classes of their society: *Tokapua* (nobles), *Tomokaka* (tradesmen) and *Tobuda* (the common people). The *Tokapua* wear special turbans and loincloths, grow their hair long and own most of the land. They used to live in walled villages built on the tops of hills both for defence and as an expression of the belief that their mythical ancestors descended onto the hilltops. Most Toraja villages are now on the plains and are surrounded by the vegetable and rice fields of the community.

The Minangkabau of West Sumatra developed more or less in isolation until their recent conversion to Islam. Theirs is a matriarchal and matrilineal society and each man or woman retains membership of his or her maternal house even after marriage. The man lives in his mother's house and visits his wife in hers. The children grow up in their mother's house and her brothers may be more familiar to them than is their own father. Similarly, the husband will assume a partial paternal role towards the children of his sisters. In his wife's house the husband holds no property and little influence whereas, in his own house he inherits through his mother and exercises control and influence over property and ritual affairs.

In Irian Jaya traditional Dani villages are composed of a number of compounds containing circular, thatched houses each set aside for a particular function. A man may have as many wives as he can afford, paying for them in pigs. Women and men sleep in separate houses within the compound. They farm their staple crop, which is the sweet potato, tobacco and other vegetables in well-irrigated and drained plots.

Although rice is the staple diet of most of the people of Indonesia and the primary village crop, there are many other traditional crops. Coconuts are grown everywhere, one sago tree will keep a family for months, fruits of all types are either cultivated or harvested in the forest, cloves and nutmeg have been immensely important trade items and vegetables are grown by every family.

Fishing is the most widespread of village activities after the growing of rice. Fish, fresh or dried, is the main source of protein for much of the population. The village economy will also be expanded by the sale of artefacts such as basketwork, carving, batik, decorative weaving, silver and jewellery.

In some isolated areas of the archipelago societies based on neolithic cultures have persisted almost unaltered until very recently; only within the last few decades

Balinese going about their daily business in the early part of the last century. Villages in Bali are based on a system of co-operative effort, with all members sharing responsibility for the organization of the community.

has the arrival of modern communications started to change them. The Sakuddei tribe on the island of Siberut off the west coast of Sumatra is a case in point. Their culture predates the introduction of rice and millet agriculture and they have no tradition of weaving, although they do keep domestic chickens and pigs. The social unit is an entity of ten to fifteen families living together in a house – the *uma* – which is itself part of the unit. Although the older men are deferred to as having more ritual knowledge and experience, there is no hierarchy and everyone, including women and children, takes part in the discussions leading to consensus.

Other neolithic survivors are the Atoni Pah Meto or 'People of the Dry Land' who are found in West Timor and have been untouched by Buddhism, Hinduism or Islam. Their social organization is the clan or *kanaf*, which is based on patrilineal descent from a common ancestor. Within the clan the unit is the *ume*, or household. The Atoni cultivate rice and their beliefs are strongly based on the cycle of sowing and harvesting.

Similarly standing aloof from centuries of outside influences are the Marind-Anim who live on the flat alluvial lands of the Merauke district in the south of Irian Jaya. This low-lying area becomes a vast swamp in the wet season. Coconuts and sago grow naturally in abundance and the Marind-Anim cultivate bananas, taro and yams. They use bamboo bows and arrows, make nets for fishing and travel in dug-out canoes up to 15 metres (50 feet) long, rowing them standing up. They decorate their bodies and practise a clan system of social order with the old men acting as the guardians of tradition and myth and the masters of ritual.

RELIGION

The professed religions of the archipelago may be officially recognized as Islam, Hinduism, Buddhism and Christianity but very much interwoven with these are far more ancient beliefs that, in some isolated inland areas, have persisted almost unchanged since neolithic times. Deeply buried in the Indonesian soul is the concept of a mystic relationship between the physical and spiritual worlds with the necessity for harmony and propitiation.

Most important to this fundamental belief are the tribal ancestors who dwell in spirit-land but are in constant communication with their living descendants. Ancestral spirits are invoked in male cult rituals where young men are taught the tribal rites and folklore in a spirit-house as part of their initiation into full adult status in the tribe. Elaborate festivals and dance are needed to reinforce the bonds with the ancestor spirits, and rituals at birth, marriage and funerals serve to ensure peace and security. Spiritual powers make themselves present in sacred drums, masks and musical instruments.

Many religious rites are concerned with the infusing of *mana*, or earthly power and authority, and the removal of *taboos*. Anyone who is perceived to be strong, wise or skilled is thought of as possessing *mana*, which implies direct access to divine powers. For instance, tribal chiefs embody the *mana* of their tribes and *mana* is present in an orator's speech. Success in warfare, skill in ritual or sorcery, fruitful wives, gardens and pigs all show *mana*.

Cannibalism of slain enemies is the ultimate way of destroying their *mana*.

Taboo or *tambu* is a system of prohibitions concerned with anything which has great *mana*. Chiefs and their families and possessions are regarded as inviolable and are set apart by privileges that protect the *mana* of their divine ancestry. Tombs, shrines, sacred stones, groves of trees and water for ritual use are all *taboo* to the unprivileged, as are offerings to the gods. *Taboos* govern agriculture, fishing, building, carving and anything else requiring the help and protection of the gods. Dangerous to *mana* are menstruating women, women in childbirth, bloodstained warriors, the sick and dying, corpses and bones of the dead.

The Javanese today profess Islam but many remnants of their prehistoric beliefs and of the ideas imported from India during the time of the Indianized kingdoms remain. Propitiation of ancestral spirits and of the evil spirits of those who died violently of murder, suicide, childbirth or cholera once required elaborate ceremonies which today in Java persist in the *selamatan*, a feast held to mark important milestones in life: birth, circumcision, marriage and death. A *selamatan* may also be held at the seventh month of pregnancy, by which time it is believed the child could survive if born prematurely. *Selamatan* have overtones of blessing, thanksgiving and grace and, when held before the start of a new undertaking or a long journey, of intercession with the gods. Mounds of yellow rice, the principle ingredient of the feast, recall the sacred mountain and seat of the Hindu gods and represent the colour of wealth and majesty. Similarly, offerings may be found left under a large Waringan tree or even at the base of traffic lights, since these are places where spirits dwell.

The Balinese came to Bali from East Java when the Hindu kingdoms were ousted by Islam. Nominally Hindu, they worship the Hindu Trinity of Brahma, Shiva and Vishnu but they also conceive of a Supreme Being, Sanghyang Widi, existing beyond good and evil, life and death, nature and the universe, as the source of all creation.

Religious rites and festivals guide the Balinese from birth to death and into the next world, and regulate every aspect of their daily life. There is no distinction between secular and religious activity. The Brahman priest, or Pedanda, who is a devotee of Shiva and may, occasionally, be a woman, carries out the ritual purifications with sanctified water. The Pemangku or village priest officiates at temple ceremonies, receiving offerings or food and flowers for the gods. Trance is recognized as a means of communication with ancestors, spirits and deities and the Balian acts as a trance medium for divine revelation. Ritual battles take place between Good represented by the Barong (a lion) and Evil represented by Rangda (a witch). These battles usually end in a compromise reflecting the balance between good and evil in the real world. Cremations take place on a propitious day, sometimes years after death, and are occasions of great ceremony and festivity, especially in the case of a grand personage.

The Dayaks of Kalimantan have had long contact with Hinduism, Buddhism and Islam but firmly retain beliefs in their own mythology. In this, the upper world is presided over by a male god, Mahatala, and the nether world by the female god, Jata. The cosmos is governed by *adat* (custom) and an equivalent of the Polynesian *taboo* operates. Shamans, who can be ritual female prostitutes or male or female transvestites, act as intermediaries between the spirit world and the people. They claim direct contact with the spirits of living persons, plants, animals and features of the environment as well as with 'master spirits' of rivers and mountains and with the ghosts of the dead.

Islam is the overwhelmingly predominant religion of Indonesia, which today has the largest Muslim population in the world – about 87 per cent of the country's 180 million people. Just under 10 per cent of the population are Christians, who are scattered in various provinces such as North Sumatra, Maluku, North Sulawesi, West Kalimantan and Irian Jaya. The majority of these are Protestant. In East Nusa Tenggara and East Timor, however, the Christian communities are predominantly Roman Catholic. Christian missionaries are still active among Indonesia's more remote settlements.

Hindus and Buddhists account for only 3 per cent of the population and most of them are found in Bali. Other provinces with significant Hindu/Buddhist communities are North Sumatra, Riau, Lampung and Central Kalimantan.

CUSTOM

Throughout Indonesia, few events in the passage of life go unaccompanied by ritual and ceremony. Activities have evolved in different ways, depending on a community's traditions, religious beliefs and the degree to which outside influences have been absorbed. Some of the most elaborate ceremonials are found among the pagan, or recently pagan, peoples of North Sumatra, Sulawesi and Irian Jaya, but it is on the Hindu island of Bali where the most complex rituals and customs of all are observed.

The basic principle of Balinese society is conformity to a collective norm, any individual divergence from which is seen to reflect on the whole community. For most people, everyday life is set within the framework of the religious calendar and regulated by the powerful dictates of social order. The rituals that ensure life-long spiritual cleanliness accompany a Balinese past each major milestone on the way to the next world.

Ceremonies involving offerings to the gods and purification with sacred water protect a new-born child when it is first allowed to touch the impure earth three months after birth. At puberty, a high-caste girl must seclude herself for three days, before ritually cleansing her body and appearing to announce her womanhood dressed in gold brocade and a crown of flowers. Also at puberty a ceremony takes place during which the front teeth of boys and girls are filed by a priest to protect against the six human frailties: lust, anger, greed, stupidity, intoxication and jealousy.

Marriage is the final initiation into adult life and into the community. Until he is married a man may not join his village association; once he is married, he must. Marriages are of two types in Bali: *mapadik*, or marriage by agreement, and *ngerorod*, or elopement. Marriage by agreement follows a formal courtship with the consent of both families, who have probably effected the introduction in the first place. Courtship involves many presents and is considered expensive. If the couple decide to elope, it is usually to a friend's house and usually the plan is well known to both families in advance. However, the girl's family is expected to create a fuss when her absence is discovered and even to send out search parties for her. On the first night of the elopement, the marriage is made official by the blessing of the priest and a small religious ceremony. Offerings are made to Ibu Partiwi, the goddess of the earth. Later the entire village will be invited to a ceremony at which the wedding will be announced to the community and the village gods. The bride then formally joins the groom's family and enters his caste.

Islam insists that burial should take place as soon as possible after death, and funeral rites are therefore not of great significance in the Muslim parts of Indonesia. In Bali, however, they are very important and result in ceremonies of great beauty and complexity. As cremation must take place on an auspicious day, and because it is extremely costly, it is often delayed for years, until a great personage is to be cremated or until a number of cremations can take place at one time. After death the body is kept in the house while friends of the deceased gather to pay their respects. On a propitious day the corpse is given temporary burial.

As the day of cremation approaches, the body is exhumed, cleaned and taken to lie in state in the courtyard of the deceased's house in a pavilion (*bale bandung*) lavishly decorated with cloths, mirrors, coloured paper beads and gilded flowers. The cremation tower, or *bade*, is a many-tiered pagoda of bamboo and paper, reminiscent of the towers of the village temples, whose base is a representation of the foundation of the world – the tortoise entwined with the sacred *naga*. A stylized figure of Garuda, the eagle, vehicle of Vishnu, also adorns the base. The number of tiers depends on the caste of the deceased: from eleven for Brahmins who are not priests to one for commoners.

The *bade* and its corpse are conveyed to the cremation site on a platform of bamboo poles carried by dozens of bearers. During the procession the platform is turned to confuse the soul so that it will not be able to find its way back to its house. At the cremation ground, the corpse is removed from the *bade*, sprinkled with holy water and placed in an elaborate sarcophagus whose decoration also denotes the status of the deceased: a cow or bull, a winged lion or a strange creature half-elephant, half-fish. Both *bade* and sarcophagus are then burnt and the ashes collected in coconut shells for transportation the next day in a procession to the sea or a large river, where they are scattered. The passage of the soul from earth to heaven cannot be complete until the cremation has taken place. Prior to that the soul lingers in limbo and cannot be completely liberated from the material world. The cremation that achieves this is, therefore, seen as a joyous occasion.

Every Balinese village has three temples around which many community festivities and holy celebrations take place. They are the *pura puseh*, the temple of origin where the village founders are honoured, the *pura desa* or village temple and the *pura dalem*, the temple of the dead. Festivals are usually confined to a village, for instance, *odalan*, the celebration of the founding of a temple, held once a Balinese year (210 days). *Galungan* is the main island-wide festival held on the Balinese new year and lasting ten days. These occasions involve everyone in the village. The ground in front of the temple resembles a fairground, with stalls for food, toys, trinkets and batik and a confusion of card games and gambling, cockfights, mystic healers, buskers, music and dancing. A *gamelan* plays in the outer court of the temple, while inside the priests carry out the religious ceremonies and purification. The women of the village, dressed in their best, bear on their heads beautiful votive offerings to be placed reverently on the altars for the benign gods, those for evil spirits being left haphazardly on the ground. In fact, offerings are an essential part of Balinese life and are found everywhere. The *ngedjot*, a small square of banana leaf on which a little rice, a flower and some chilli are placed, is set in the courtyard of every house and renewed early every morning.

In Java, the long influence of Islam has done away with the Hindu and pre-Hindu ceremonies and festivals which preceded it, although vestiges remain. The *selamatan* is one such. In Yogyakarta, *sekatan* is a festival to celebrate the Prophet Mohammed's birthday but is clearly an Islamic overlay on an earlier indigenous rite. A special *gamelan* which normally lives in the Kraton Mosque is brought to the Great Mosque. Some days later, a procession of the prince's troops, palace retainers and subjects escorts the *gamelan* back to the Kraton, after which

coconut – *kelapa muda* – has a green husk with a layer of soft flesh inside and a lot of very light, refreshing watery milk which is often drunk straight from the fruit. As the coconut matures, the milk becomes thicker and the flesh denser. The milk is used as a tenderizer for meat and poultry or mixed with brightly coloured syrup and the scooped-out soft flesh to make a garishly coloured and extremely sweet drink. Later, as the flesh continues to firm, it is used for all sorts of sticky cakes and sweets. A juice squeezed from the grated flesh, known as *santen*, is used throughout Indonesia to add flavour to dishes and act as a thickener.

Among other essential ingredients is soy sauce, called *kecap* in Indonesian (from which the English word 'ketchup' derives). *Kecap asin*, which is thin and salty, and *kecap manis*, which is black, thick and much sweeter, approximate to the 'young' and 'old' soy sauce to be found in Chinese supermarkets the world over. *Terasi*, an extremely powerful paste made from prawns which have fermented in the sun, is used ground up with other spices in a variety of curries and other dishes. Chillies, another introduction from South America, come in all sizes but the general rule is the smaller the hotter, the seeds being the hottest part. They are used either fresh or dried.

Natural local spices and flavours include candlenuts, cardamom, cinnamon, cloves, ginger, galingale, lemon grass, lemon leaves, nutmeg, screwpine leaves, pepper, tamarind and turmeric, all of which can be found laid out in the market for your inspection.

Fruit

Many wonderful tropical fruits are grown in Indonesia such as pineapples, bananas (over forty types), lichees, mangoes and papayas. The justly famous durian is a large fruit covered with extremely hard and sharp pyramidal spikes which, when cut open, reveals four or five white segments each containing a seed. The smell is powerful and the taste is regarded as delicious. Indonesians and many foreigners love it to distraction but the managers of hotels and airlines will not allow it on the premises. Mangosteens are the size of an orange with a hard, dark brown skin and sweet white flesh. The juice from the skin when it is broken open will stain clothes for ever. The rambutan is a golfball-sized fruit covered with a soft hairy skin with sweet, white fragrant flesh and a central stone. Salak, from Bali, is a small, pear-shaped brown fruit with a shiny scaly skin and rather uninteresting waxy flesh. Papaya, originally from Central and South America, looks ridiculous when growing as the big green fruits stick out from the top of a bare trunk with a frieze of leaves above. The flesh, cold from the refrigerator and with a squeeze of lime, is an unsurpassed breakfast fruit. Jackfruit, pomelo and starfruit are also common.

Cooking

Indonesian meals are founded on a staple dish plus dried fish, chillies and soup. Dishes of vegetables are added where possible, as is meat. Noodles and fried rice – *nasi goreng*, introduced from China – are popular everywhere.

Raw ingredients are bought daily in the market and are usually prepared and cooked by the mistress of the house. Cooking traditionally takes place outside the house on a charcoal or wood-fired stove or brazier-like device, though now many houses have kitchens with electric or gas stoves. There are few cookery books and each family will have its own way of preparing a dish which is passed on by word of mouth and example to the next generation.

Java

Javanese cooking is greatly influenced by the island's long period of Hinduism and close contact with India. However, this influence is now so assimilated as to be almost unrecognizable as distinctly foreign. The Chinese influence is much more recent but extremely pervasive, particularly in the towns where noodles and fried rice would be perceived by most people as Indonesian. The Dutch contributed to the Indonesian love of sticky cakes and sweets and in the 1920s they concocted that extraordinary dish the *Rijstaffel*. Originally created to satisfy the vast Sunday lunch appetites of the Dutch planters, it has become a sort of national tourist meal, usually now consisting of a large array of lavish ingredients in highly spiced sauces with a central bowl of rice.

Chicken is widely used in Java in curries, fried and in other spiced dishes. Soya bean curd – *tofu* – is rich in protein and is eaten with sauces or fried. It also appears in fresh fruit salads. Another soya bean derivative is *tempe* which is made by allowing the boiled beans to ferment to produce a cake which is then boiled or fried. It is high in protein but rather uninteresting. Rice rolls, known as *lemper*, are delicious. *Satay* of chicken or

A street vendor offers his wares, Java, 1903. Balanced on his bamboo pole are a portable brazier and a selection of simple foods to be prepared on the spot.

lamb is popular served with a peanut sauce and *lontong*.

Bali

Most of Bali is infertile and, as a result, sparsely populated. What most tourists see is the south-eastern corner where the soil is fertile and the people rich. Here food and ritual go hand in hand and offerings of food and produce are to be seen balanced on the heads of Balinese ladies on their way to the temples on any festival day. Bali rears a very small form of beef cattle whose meat is exceptionally tender and sweet but the two most typically Balinese dishes use duck and pork. *Babi guling*, or roast sucking pig, is cooked whole on a spit over a charcoal fire. *Bebek betutu* is a local duck stuffed with cassava leaves flavoured with a large assortment of spices.

Sumatra

Sumatra is an island of contrasts: in the extreme north is the province of Aceh which is fiercely Muslim and independent; further south the Bataks were until recently animists but are now predominantly Christian; further south again the lush, wet lands of Central and South Sumatra are also Muslim but much more relaxed than Aceh. These differences are reflected in the food. In Aceh, of course, there is no pork, and the food shows a close affinity with that of Arabia, where many of its inhabitants originated, and of India, as the province was the first landfall of those arriving from the West. Batak food is totally distinct, using herbs and plants found only in the Batak highlands. Pork is very much in evidence and dog meat is considered a delicacy. In the central and southern parts of the island the food becomes hotter (in the chilli sense) and, although pork is not eaten, much more meat is used than in Java. One famous dish is *rendang*, traditionally made with buffalo meat cut into cubes and cooked in coconut milk spiced with chillies, lemon grass, garlic and turmeric.

Sulawesi

Here, again, is a divide: between Christian Manado in the extreme north, where pork is common but also rats, mice, bats and dog meat may be found on the table, and the rest of the island which is more or less Muslim. Food is often cooked in the open section of a sawn-off length of green bamboo which is stuck upright into the ground in front of a charcoal fire and turned during cooking. The result is moist and flavoured by the bamboo.

Kalimantan

The island of Borneo, which Indonesia shares with the Malaysian states of Sarawak and Sabah and with wealthy Brunei, is historically underpopulated, with the scattered communities strung out along the rivers practising slash-and-burn cultivation of basic staples and vegetables. Fish is the main source of protein with wild boar and, more recently, domesticated pig – a meat for high days and holidays. Turtle eggs, which look rather like squashed ping-pong balls, are eaten boiled. However, most of the present-day population is made up either of transmigrants from Java or people working in or for the oil and gas industries. These people bring the cooking of their origins with them and adapt it so far as is necessary to use the available ingredients. It is fair to say that Kalimantan has no cuisine of its own.

Maluku

Lying far to the east, Maluku is much drier than the big islands of Borneo, Java and Sumatra. The islands are also very small and surrounded by a provident sea. The diet, then, depends very largely on fish and, because rice is difficult to grow, the staples are dry-weather crops such as sago, taro and yams as well as the non-indigenous sweet potato and cassava which were introduced by the Portuguese. When a mature sago palm will produce enough sago for a family for four months, there is naturally little incentive to grow more difficult crops. Maize and breadfruit are also common, and coconuts and bananas are everywhere. The islands of Maluku are, of course, the spice islands from which cloves and nutmeg, the spices over which the Europeans fought for so long, once came. This trade is now less important than it was and, surprisingly, the local inhabitants have traditionally made little use in their cooking of the spices they grew.

Eating Out

At the simplest level of the catering business in Indonesia is the street vendor with a hand cart or large containers suspended from the ends of a bamboo pole. He may have a portable charcoal brazier on which he can fry noodles or grill *satay*; he may specialize in residential districts where his traditional cry will bring housewives out to buy from him or he may frequent the business districts where office workers can stand beside his barrow to eat.

Next in line and also found throughout Indonesia is the *warung*, a temporary, portable restaurant consisting of a roof of canvas or corrugated iron, no walls but perhaps a canvas screen, a bench or two, a table and a counter. Delicious if simple food is served at astonishingly low prices.

Outside the major cities Chinese restaurants are found fairly widely, as are the Padang-style restaurants serving food from Padang in West Sumatra, almost on the Equator. Padang food, spicy and hot, comes to the table unasked in numerous little bowls of different meat, fish, poultry and vegetable dishes. Customers eat what they like and pay only for what they eat.

In the big cities restaurants abound but rarely serve Indonesian food. Japanese, Thai, American, French, Italian and many other cuisines can be found in cities like Jakarta and Surabaya but the Indonesian food offered in hotel restaurants is likely to be disappointing. Local people usually prefer to eat at home.

Drinks

Tea and coffee are the universal drinks of Indonesia. Both grow in the country and the coffee has a very high international reputation. *Kopi tubruk* is made with freshly ground coffee and is usually rather gritty but the flavour is excellent. A variety of fruit drinks and violently coloured soft drinks is available everywhere. *Es cendol* is a cold, sweet drink made from coconut milk, rice flour, sugar syrup and ice.

Most of Indonesia being, nominally at least, Muslim, alcohol is not readily available and is very expensive. The exceptions to this are the rice and palm wines brewed in the non-Muslim areas of the country and a beer of Dutch origin – *Bintang Baru* – which is fairly widely available even in small *warungs*. It is usually warm and will often have ice added to the glass. Rice wine – *brem* – from Bali and palm wine – *tuak* – in Sulawesi and Kalimantan, vary in taste from smooth and pleasant to harsh and, sometimes, lethally strong. The Dayak people of Kalimantan also brew a rice wine of innocuous taste but alarming potency. Muslim Indonesians tend to be relaxed about alcohol, particularly in the cities, and almost anything you want can be had in the Chinese stalls in the markets.

THE PERFORMING ARTS

MUSIC

The most famous music of Indonesia must be that of the *gamelan* orchestra, whether of Java or of Bali. One of the first westerners to comment on it was Sir Francis Drake, in 1580, who recorded in the log of the *Golden Hind* that he had heard music 'of a very strange kind, yet the sound was pleasant and delightfull'. Sir Thomas Stamford Raffles sent back to London a set of *gamelan* instruments at the beginning of the 19th century and at the Grand Universal Exhibition of 1889 in Paris there were performances by Javanese players and dancers on a *gamelan* from Cirebon which had been presented to the Paris Conservatoire a couple of years before. It was these performances which Claude Debussy found so enthralling and which were to have considerable influence on some of his subsequent works.

The majority of *gamelan* instruments are made of metal – usually bronze but occasionally iron. These divide into two groups: metallophones, and gongs with central knobs or bosses. In addition there are hand drums, an end-blown bamboo flute and a two-stringed *rebab*, or fiddle, of Arabic origin. All the instruments except the *rebab* and the hand drums are struck by a variety of mallets, and this style of playing gives the gamelan its name: *-an*, the striking action of *gamel*, a hammer.

The *gamelan* can be played in two modes, loud and soft, and in two tunings, *slendro* and *pelog*. The *slendro* tuning is a pentatonic scale, having five notes and no semi-tones. The difference between this and the black notes on a piano is that the intervals are more or less equal, whereas the black notes on a piano have clear differences between whole tones and minor thirds. The *pelog* tuning has seven notes though not all are always used. In both cases the intervals between the notes are not precisely equal and each *gamelan* will have its own personality depending on how it is tuned. This tuning, or *embat*, is considered very important and allows a sharp ear to distinguish one *gamelan* from another. Since the instruments (with the exception of the *rebab*) cannot be retuned, a full Javanese *gamelan* has many of its instruments duplicated – one in the *slendro* tuning and one in the *pelog*.

The gongs are all circular and are struck on their central protruding boss. The larger ones are suspended vertically from a bar and are struck with a round-headed, padded mallet. The smaller gongs are supported horizontally on cords strung across a wooden frame with the central boss uppermost, and are played by hitting the boss with sticks lightly padded with string wound round them. The gongs provide the structural framework of the music and the embellishment and infilling.

The *saran* family of bronze metallophone plates over a wooden resonator, and their cousins the *slentem*, in which the plates are suspended over tuned bamboo resonators, are the crucial instruments of the *gamelan*: they provide the nuclear melody of the piece from which the parts of all the other instruments can be deduced. There is also a xylophone called the *gambang* whose plates are made of hardwood, struck by round disks mounted on the ends of horn sticks. It is an embellishing instrument. The flute and the *rebab* have considerable rhythmic elasticity and are used with the (usually female) human voice for ornamentation.

The Balinese *gamelan* is superficially the same as the Javanese but, in fact, the ensembles are different and the music pronouncedly so. The Balinese *gamelan* underwent a revolution early in the last century when a new form of playing and dancing called *kebyar* evolved. This is much more exuberant than the more courtly and dignified music of Central Java. Unpadded wooden mallets give a brighter, louder and more 'tinkly' sound to the metallophones than the padded mallets of Java.

In Sulawesi a xylophone orchestra of plates mounted on wooden frames without any resonators is played most often at harvest time. Flutes are played all over the archipelago, together with a variety of drums and stringed instruments like the two-stringed *hasapi* of the Toba Batak and the *sapeh* of the Dayaks which is a flat lute with rattan strings. The Dayaks of the interior of Kalimantan have an ancient instrument known since the Bronze Age, called a *kledi*, which can be seen on the bas-reliefs of Borobudur. It is a gourd with six or eight bamboo canes sticking out of it and it is played like a mouth organ.

DANCE DRAMAS

The great dance dramas of Java are based on the two ancient Indian works, the *Mahabharata* and the *Ramayana*. The origins and date of the *Mahabharata* are unknown but it is thought to have been considered a venerable collection of traditional verse even in the 4th century AD, telling of a mythical battle fought in North India in the 13th or 14th century BC. The *Ramayana* is attributed to the poet Valmiki, who may have written it in the 3rd or 4th century AD. It is essentially a love story, the search by Prince Rama for his faithful wife, Sita.

In Bali the *Ramayana* and *Mahabharata* epics are also well known but they are performed in addition to a number of other dance dramas which have their roots either in Java, where they have since died out under Muslim pressure, or in pre-Hindu rituals. In Java classical dance tends to be the preserve of the courts, whereas in Bali dance, music and drama are totally interwoven with everyday life. Performances take place outdoors in a village or in a temple forecourt. The dancers and musicians will be ordinary people who go about their normal tasks during the day and perform in the evening at festivals or other occasions. Only the teachers of music and dance will call that their occupation.

There are hundreds of dance dramas in Bali, many of which are continually evolving. Among the most famous are the *Kecak*, *Barong* and *Legong* dances. The *Kecak* performance includes an inspired use of the human voice as up to 150 men, seated in concentric rings on the ground, produce a complex rhythmic sound capable of registering a wide range of emotions. There is no *gamelan*. At the very centre of the rings an episode from the *Ramayana* will be enacted. This is often some part of the epic involving Hanuman from which the dance gets its other name – the Monkey Dance.

The *Barong* dance is essentially a performance symbolizing the conflict of good and evil. The evil is personified by the demon witch, Rangda, with ferocious mask, lolling fiery tongue, pendulous breasts and rolling eyes. She represents the night, darkness, sickness and death while her opponent, the Barong, in the shape of a lion, represents day, light, the sun and the force which overcomes evil. During the concluding battle, the dancers rush to the aid of the Barong but are put under a spell by Rangda so that they turn their *kris* on themselves. In performance it seems that blood must flow but, when the dancers are released from their trance by the village priest who sprinkles holy water over them with the Barong's beard at the end, they are always found to be unharmed.

The *Legong* is the most feminine and graceful of the common Balinese dances. The cast consists of the two Legong, young girls who are trained from the age of four or five and retire at puberty, and a palace attendant. The Legong are dressed identically in great splendour and they dance together either in total unison or in a mirror image of each other. A *dalang*, or narrator, explains the story as it unfolds and the dance is accompanied by a *gamelan*.

Two male solo dances are the *Baris* and the *Kebyar*. The *Baris* is a traditional war-dance which originally formed the dedication of a Balinese warrior and his weapon to the gods. The *Kebyar* is a solo male equivalent of the *Legong* in which the dancer mirrors the moods of the *gamelan* in his dancing. One of the most strenuous and subtle of the Balinese dances, it is said that the dancer must be able to play every instrument in the *gamelan* in order to be able to convey the nuances of the music in his performance.

Dances are performed all over Indonesia though rarely reaching the levels of sophistication of the court dances of Java and Bali. Many are primitive round dances, long pre-dating Hindu and Muslim influences, though they have generally absorbed elements of them. Only in Irian Jaya has the primitive neolithic dance survived. Many dances are connected with funerals and warfare, such as those of the Toraja, the Bataks and the Dayaks of Kalimantan.

Village orchestra in Java. A local music group such as this will be kept busy throughout the year performing at religious festivals and community celebrations.

WAYANG KULIT

Wayang is a term used to denote any type of theatrical performance ranging from western dramas to *wayang kulit*, a form of shadow-play using fretworked puppets. *Kulit* means leather, the material from which the puppets are made.

Opinion is divided as to whether the *wayang kulit* is derived from the shadow dramas of South India or whether it is an independent evolution from ancient indigenous initiation rites. It is also called *wayang purwa*, where *purwa* means ancient. The earliest reference to what was probably *wayang kulit* is found in an inscription of King Balitung in 907 AD. Javanese translations of the *Ramayana* and the *Mahabharata* were available then and performances were of a sacred nature as offerings to the gods for fertility and to propitiate the ancestral spirits.

The *wayang kulit* uses flat puppets whose shadows are projected onto a screen of white cloth by a lamp. The puppeteer, or *dalang*, sits behind the screen in front of the lamp, while the audience may sit either in front of the screen watching the shadows or on the same side as the *dalang*, where the colour of the puppets can be appreciated.

The *gamelan* is positioned behind the *dalang* and traditionally plays in the *slendro* tuning. The musicians sing or clap in addition to playing their instruments. Female singers are a introduction of the 20th century but now one or two of these *pesinden* are thought essential and there may be as many as 25. The songs are not necessarily related to the action of the play, nor do the female singers represent the female characters. The songs may be used for effect, to break up the main performance or to get across some current message.

There may be 400 flat puppets in a set owned by a wealthy or royal patron, although only about 60 are normally used in any one performance. They are made out of buffalo parchment which is tooled and punched and then painted and gilded. The figures are normally only jointed at shoulder and elbow, and are manipulated by polished bone handles and supported by horn rods with sharpened ends. Each puppet is a highly stylized exaggeration of a type, having its own character and being instantly recognizable to a *wayang* lover. Important figures may be represented by a number of puppets during a performance, each demonstrating the particular mood of the character at the time.

Performances usually start at about nine o'clock in the evening and, at dawn, when the last great battle has been fought and good has prevailed, a three-dimensional puppet is introduced to dance before the victorious shadow puppets and bring the performance to an end.

The *dalang* is the master of the *wayang kulit*. His is a long and arduous training during which he must memorize an enormous repertory. The *dalang* selects, anchors and manipulates the puppets, he must be able to recite Javanese poetry, make formal declarations and speak the partially improvised dialogue of his characters in as many as thirty different voices. He extemporizes (often in Bahasa Indonesia) the earthy dialogue of the *panakawan*, the clowns. He can use this element of the performance to comment on local affairs, promote a campaign (for example, birth control) or make attacks on the government which would be unacceptable in normal society. He is traditionally immune from any retribution for critical remarks.

Wayang kulit puppets are traditionally made by families, the more skilled members doing the difficult bits while others, even children, do the easy bits. Fine puppets can be bought from the Sagio workshop in Gendeng outside Yogyakarta and in the village of Mayaran near Surakarta. Surakarta's royal palace workshop can also be visited.

WAYANG GOLEK

Wayang golek are fully three-dimensional puppets with wooden, articulated arms and a head which rotates on the central support rod running up through the body of the puppet, concealed by its clothes. Although the Batak of North Sumatra have an articulated puppet called *Si Galegale*, which is used to perform complicated dances at the funerals of people who die without children, and is clearly very ancient, the *wayang golek* of Java and Bali probably developed on the north coast of Java and were modelled on the *wayang kulit* puppets. There is greater freedom of design in the *wayang golek* puppets than in the more stylized *wayang kulit*. The arms are articulated at the shoulder and elbow and controlled by thin rods attached to the hands. Operated by a skilled *dalang*, the puppets can appear uncannily life-like.

Although these puppet shows are found all over Java, they are particularly popular in West Java where the preferred performances are those based on the Hindu epics, the *Ramayana* and *Mahabharata*. In Central Java the *wayang kulit* monopolizes the Hindu epic performances, with *wayang golek* presenting an Islamic cycle of stories based on the heroic adventures of Mohammed's uncle, Amir Hamza. These stories are set in exotic locations, with European kings in 18th-century dress and dashing Arabian knights engaged in intrigue and trials of strength with each other and various *jinn* or Middle Eastern minor demons.

Throughout Java these puppets are being used more and more in non-traditional ways with modern, cigarette-smoking characters, motor-cycle riders and soldiers complete with rifles taking part in performances of comic realism which may also be used to get across a political or social message.

As with the *wayang kulit* tradition, the making of the *wayang golek* puppets tends to be handed down in families from generation to generation. The master puppet-maker will perform the rituals appropriate to starting work on a powerful demon or deity and will be responsible for carving the head in a strong, light wood such as *arbasiah*. Other members of the family will carve the rest of the body, attach the rods and sew the clothing. Central Javanese puppets are sold in the markets of Yogyakarta and Surakarta and may be commissioned from the master mask-maker and puppet-maker, Pak Warnowiskito, of Krantil outside Yogyakarta. In West Java, *wayang golek* puppets are on sale in Bandung and Bogor as well as in many villages. The road up to the *Puncak*, a popular weekend hill resort on the way to Bandung, is lined outside the town with stalls selling puppets (among much else).

WAYANG TOPENG

Wayang topeng, or mask drama, is one of the oldest performing arts in Indonesia. In fact, the use of masks in dance and ritual is time-honoured throughout the world. In the ancient Melanesian religions, masks are the most important man-made objects. They may have originated as death masks or as a means of visually dramatizing the presence of powerful ancestors and deities, on whom the security of the community depends, while rendering the mask wearer impersonal. They are often housed in shrines *taboo* to the uninitiated and their display is accompanied by dancing, music, song and feasting. They may be destroyed after use. In the Asmat villages of Irian Jaya relatives of a dead person impersonate him for a day wearing string masks, while in Kalimantan the Dayak peoples have masks of animals and dragons painted in white, black and red which are worn with hornbill feathers and capes of leaves at rituals to ensure a good crop. In Lombok, the Islamic *sasak* peoples use masked drama to exorcise pestilence.

In Java and Bali the use of *wayang*

topeng as entertainment is said to have been invented by Sunan Kalijaga, one of the nine *wali sanga*, or saints, of Java's north coast cities in the 16th century. Certainly *wayang topeng* is taken very seriously today in Cirebon on that coast. In Java masks are used for history plays about Javanese kings as well as for plays taken from the Hindu epics. They are also used in trance dances in places such as the Dieng Plateau. A rare use of a ritual mask in a post-Islamic setting is the masked leader of the *sekaten* procession to mark the Prophet Mohammed's birthday in Yogyakarta. Balinese masks such as the Borong and Rangda masks blend into costume, and the Borong may owe something to the Chinese ceremonial lion in this respect. Balinese masked dances are often based on historical tales, sometimes with one dancer assuming a number of masks as the performance proceeds and sometimes with a troupe of masked dancers. Masks are usually kept high up in the village Temple of the Dead, wrapped in a cloth.

Sacred masks in Bali are often made by high-caste families with a specialist knowledge of the appropriate rituals. The facial features are firmly established by tradition. Before cutting the living wood for a powerful mask the permission of the tree growing in a sacred place such as a graveyard or temple courtyard should be sought. Pigs' teeth or sea shells may be used to form the teeth, and human or horsehair used for the hair of the coarser characters. The more refined characters tend to have their hair painted on. Javanese masks are leaner and more stylized than those of Bali, which also have rounder lips and less receding chins. Those of Cirebon have flatter faces and those of East Java and Madura are more heavily carved. The best mask-makers in Bali are to be found around the village of Mas and marvellous masks are produced by the puppet-maker Pak Warnowiskito of Krantil near Yogyakarta.

WAYANG WONG

Wayang wong, or *wayang orang*, is dance and drama played out by men and women, without masks, speaking their own lines. A *dalang* is usually present in traditional dance to comment on the action but his role is much less important than in the other forms of *wayang* where the performers or puppets are mute. *Wayang wong* is an important part of the court ritual of Central Java and rulers themselves have often been enthusiastic dancers and choreographers. Performances may last several days and involve the ruler, his family and friends, and court retainers as well as the permanent corps of dancers and musicians. Javanese court dance is very reserved and is said to have originated in the 19th century out of the masked dances of the courts. Dance groups tend to be either male or female, with the women's movements being very restrained and composed.

Major *wayang wong* performances of the *Ramayana* take place by moonlight over four successive nights each month during the dry season, before the floodlit façade of the Prambanan Temple outside Yogyakarta. There are other, less formal dances such as that in which up to eight dancers riding horses made of plaited bamboo become possessed by evil spirits and have to be recalled by incense and incantations administered by a mystic teacher. These are the traditional, stylized dances of the great Javanese courts and of Bali. In Java and elsewhere all over Indonesia strolling players give extempore performances of much simpler tales, often with much humour and informality.

CONTEMPORARY THEATRE

Throughout Indonesia travelling players have traditionally moved from village to village performing their own versions of folk tales. These performances are generally rudimentary since the players have no time to rehearse and few props or costumes. However, the tales are usually well known to the audience and the injection of local colour, humour and, sometimes, a political message makes them very popular. Unfortunately, the practice is dying out in the face of universal radio and increasingly universal television.

Jakarta and Yogyakarta are the biggest centres for modern theatre as it is known in the West. In Jakarta there are three major theatres, the Taman Ismail Marzuki, the Gedung Kesenian and the Jakarta Convention Centre. In Yogyakarta there are the Gedung Senisono, Gedung Kredisono Bulak Sumur and the Bulakgunu Student Centre.

Of the current writers and directors, Rendra, who owns the Bengkel Teater in Yogyakarta, is probably the best known outside Indonesia. He is an experimental director who has attracted a large following over the years. His work is often a trenchant criticism of social and political abuse. Other writer/directors are Arifin C. Noor of Teater Kecil, Ikranagara of Teater Saja and Putu Widjaja, all of whom comment more or less unfavourably on current affairs. Musical comedy is very popular in Jakarta and three famous companies are Teater Gandrik, Teater Gapit and Opera Kacoa (which means cockroach!).

ARTS AND CRAFTS

ARCHITECTURE

The architecture of Indonesia falls into various categories. The traditional house, or *rumah adat*, has evolved from very early origins to take account of the spiritual, social and religious life of the community as well as the climate. Except in Java and Bali, almost all traditional houses are built on stilts either on dry land or over shallow water. The main structure of the house is of hardwood with various types of cladding. The torrential monsoon rains of most of the country have dictated a very steeply pitched roof, often with the lower part of the slope markedly less steep to throw the water away from the foundations of the building. The ancient peoples of the Minangkabau and Toraja build houses with vast upswept roofs within which the actual living area may be quite small. Windows are usually small or non-existent.

The Malay model house is found in the coastal regions of the country and its layout is adapted to the requirements of the Islamic faith. It has few rooms but they tend to be light and airy, with generous windows to take advantage of coastal breezes. It, too, is built on stilts with a steeply pitched roof, but without the exaggerated prow and stern of the Minangkabau. A modular building system has developed which allows a house to be easily adapted to suit the size of the family.

As a general rule, only in Java and Bali are traditional houses built directly on the ground. In Java a low stone foundation plinth is sometimes used as a base for the timber pillars which support the roof;

cladding is often just a mat of woven split bamboo attached to the main pillars. Roofs are thatched and usually have four slopes from the centre. These days, corrugated metal sheeting is the standard. The Balinese family lives in a walled compound containing a number of small structures which include the family temple, the rice store, separate sleeping accommodation for parents and unmarried girls and for adults, and a kitchen. The rice store is the only structure on stilts.

In Irian Jaya and the other eastern outer islands, variations of the thatched conical house are found. The Dayak longhouse of Kalimantan has already been described on page 28.

The Dutch houses which are found throughout Indonesia are built of stuccoed brick with tiled roofs. Each was required to occupy a minimum percentage of its site, so that the colonial districts of the Indonesian cities differ from those of Malaysia or India in being much less crowded and more airy. The Dutch believed that the air was responsible for much of the disease in cities like

Jakarta and Surabaya, so windows tend to be small and balconies rare.

Traditional Chinese town houses are built in terraces and are typically long and thin, running from the front entrance in the main street to a lane at the rear. Immediately inside is a public room with the altar to the ancestors or, in the case of a shophouse, the shop. Houses are usually of two storeys with bedrooms, bathrooms and storerooms arranged over the front room and round an interior courtyard. Larger and more opulent Chinese houses consist of a series of halls parallel to the front hall with a rear courtyard or garden, around which are the living quarters, servants' quarters, kitchens and storerooms. The whole is surrounded by a high wall.

Today, of course, the big cities of Jakarta, Surabaya, Medan and Bandung bear all the marks of modern international architecture: high-rise offices and condominiums, residential estates with each house set in a little garden, supermarkets, multi-carriageway roads, flyovers and traffic congestion to match.

Decoration

Much of the traditional architecture of Indonesia is left unadorned except for some wood fretting or such things as scalloped eaves. However, there are exceptions, the most dramatic of which are to be found in Bali, Sumatra and Sulawesi.

The public buildings, palaces and temples of Bali are made of soft stone or brick which is easily carved. Elaborate doorways, many metres high, and temple walls are carved with an intricate lace of symbolic motifs and representations of gods and demons. The master carver knows the ritual positions of all these sculptures and will augment them with personal carvings in inconspicuous corners. Free-standing statues of demons and divinities mounted on pedestals are found in temple courtyards. The diversity of the carvings is amazing and springs from many inspirations, both Hindu and local.

The Minangkabau construct houses and public buildings with graceful, upswept roofs rising to slender pinnacles at the gables. The walls and gables are of intricately carved and painted wood whose

Thatched house raised on a sturdy timber framework, Lombok, 1911. Except in Java and Bali, traditional houses throughout Indonesia are rarely built directly on the ground.

Opposite: *The striking upswept roof of this Minangkabau house in Sumatra, photographed in the 1920s, is typical of the region. The building on the right is for storing rice.*

motifs and colours may have been derived from Chinese brocades. Many beautiful old houses are still to be seen around Bukittinggi. The Batak roof is much heavier than the Minangkabau and without the pinnacles. It sits much lower on the substructure but here, too, the gables are carved and painted and there are brightly coloured screens of split bamboo. The ends of the ridges may be ornamented with horned buffalo skulls. The island of Samosir in Lake Toba still has some fine traditional houses.

The Toraja people of Central Sulawesi also decorate their houses, public buildings and rice barns. The colours used are those symbolizing human life (red), purity (white), God's blessing (yellow) and death (black). The wooden gable ends and wall panels are incised with spiral and geometric designs into which the colour is rubbed and 'fixed' with the local palm wine. Motifs representing fertility, prosperity and power are customarily incorporated into the designs decorating the houses of nobles in this highly hierarchical society. It is in Toraja, above all, that the great ceremonial feast held on the completion of a building is a symbol of the power, both spiritual and temporal, of its owner.

Outside traditional architecture, the modern architecture of the cities and the imported styles of the Chinese and Dutch, lie the immensely important groups of stone-built monuments erected in the 8th, 9th and 10th centuries in Central and East Java. Of these, Borobudur is the greatest, followed closely by its near neighbour, the Prambanan. Also on the Plain of Kedu are numerous other interesting *candi*, or temples, from the same period. In addition there is a series of very early *candi* on the Dieng Plateau, north of Wonosobo, dating from the beginning of the 9th century. They stand at 2,000 metres (6,500 feet) above sea level among swirling mists and bubbling sulphurous springs. In East Java there are a number of interesting stone and brick temples from the 13th and 14th centuries which can be reached from Surabaya or from the charming hill town of Malang.

Borobudur

Borobudur was built some time around AD 800 on the foundation of a natural hill. It is a portrait in stone of the Mahayana Buddhist cosmic world as well as a representation of the sacred mountain inhabited by the gods. The immense, square edifice is surrounded by galleries which portray, on the lowest levels, the delights and tribulations of earthly life. Next are a series of galleries telling the story of the life of Prince Siddhartha on his way to becoming the Gautama Buddha, his previous incarnations and episodes from the life of the Bodisattava Sudhana. Above these the form becomes circular, with three terraces of openwork *stupas* – bell-shaped memorial shrines – each containing a statue of the Buddha. The topmost terrace represents the attainment of formlessness and total abstraction.

Apart from the beauty of the temple as a whole, the nearly 1,500 bas-relief panels carved on the walls of the galleries are a fascinating record of daily and courtly life in Central Java at the beginning of the 9th century. Ships and elephants, dancing girls and scenes of homage, agricultural scenes, fishing, hunting and warfare are all portrayed as contemporary vignettes. The Borobudur complex has been the subject of a now complete ten-year-plus restoration programme by UNESCO which virtually dismantled the monument, labelled and cleaned every stone, laid reinforced concrete foundations and then re-assembled the whole jigsaw puzzle.

Prambanan

The other great temple complex in Central Java, also recently restored, was built in the latter part of the 9th century and so is slightly later than Borobudur. It is a Hindu monument of eight major *candi* on a raised platform. The largest, dedicated to Shiva, is over 45 metres (150 feet) high and is flanked by two slightly smaller *candi* dedicated to Brahma and Vishnu. Facing these three are *candi* dedicated to Nandi, the bull

mount of Shiva, the swan of Brahma and Garuda, the vehicle of Vishnu. All are vitally carved with scenes from the *Ramayana* and various half-human, half-bird heavenly beings, lions, trees of heaven, demons and minor deities. Two small temples on this upper terrace were, perhaps, treasuries. A lower terrace contains many other buildings.

ART

Art, in the sense of fine art painting, was not common in Indonesia until the 20th century. Of course painted masks, puppets and other artefacts go back a very long way, but the concept of painting as a picture is modern. The only exception might be the beautifully illustrated manuscripts which were produced in Java and Bali from around the end of the 18th century. Many of the manuscripts of Hindu epics and Javanese poems are beautifully decorated with lively scenes from the text. High ranking people are usually shown in profile in the stylized manner of the

wayang kulit, whereas the common people are treated with much less formality. The size of the characters very often reflects their relative status. There are also letter-headings from the courts in various parts of Indonesia, such as that on the letter from Sultan Iskandar Muda of Aceh to King James I in 1615. The majority of Indonesian texts were not illustrated, however. Today there are flourishing schools of painting in many parts of Indonesia, particularly in Yogyakarta where probably the best known Indonesian artist, Affandi, works.

Traditional Balinese art consisted of astrological calendars with auspicious days noted, or hangings for temples or palaces. The paintings were usually on cloth and in the *wayang* style: that is, a shallow, two-dimensional style reminiscent of the *wayang kulit*. Only a few specified shades of blue, brown, yellow and red could be used. The paintings were mostly illustrations of Hindu epics and literature with the main picture

Built around AD 800, Borobudur in Central Java is the largest Buddhist monument in the world. This enormous stone complex, with its shrines and statues, and spectacularly carved galleries and terraces, is an eternal reminder of the path to enlightenment.

divided up into a series of single scene episodic cartoons, each bordered with flames, walls or other decorative devices. The great and the good are shown in elegant form and dress, bedecked with jewels, while the giants and demons are shown in ungainly postures with distended bellies and bulging eyes. Klungkung is still a centre for this style of painting and the painted roof of the Hall of Justice there is an excellent example.

As temple and courtly patronage began to wane during the early years of the 20th century, Balinese artists started to adapt their work to make it more attractive to the western tourists who were beginning to flood into Bali. Two European painters who had a dramatic effect on Balinese painting were Walter Spies and Rudolf Bonnet, who arrived in Bali in the 1930s to live and work. They donated Western artists' materials to the local artists of Ubud, Batuan, Mas and Sanur, and a new style of art arose in which paintings were created for their own value rather than as decorative coverings. Single scene paintings of everyday life in the rice fields or markets became popular. These works still showed their traditional origins but became much freer and more varied in colour. They were full of detail – no corner of the canvas was left uncovered by meticulously drawn figures, trees, animals and other aspects of rural life. This movement became known as the Pita Maha School.

The next development again took place with the encouragement of two European artists, Aries Smit and Hans Snell, who, in the 1960s, helped to found what is known as the Young Artists Group in Ubud. Still working within the Balinese tradition, colours became far brighter, the scenes more animated and the drawing, perhaps, less fine. Today, Balinese paintings continue to portray modern rural life, including among their subjects tourists with cameras, aeroplanes and motor bikes. Good examples of all styles can be seen in the Museum Neka at Campuan, which is on the outskirts of Ubud.

LITERATURE

Indonesia's ancient legends, myths, stories and tribal histories were transmitted orally for centuries, as in all other parts of the world. Professional storytellers moved about from one village to another until very recently. The *wayang* performances also transmitted the old tales from generation to generation. The earliest written records were engraved on stones or on 'paper' made from the leaves of the Lontar palm.

The most ancient dated documents were written in the 5th century and deal with grants of land and other administrative matters. However interesting, they cannot be called literature. The earliest examples of literature were adaptations of the great Indian epics and poetic works, known as *kakawins*, in the formal style of the Indian *kavyas*. The earliest of these *kakawins* is the *Arjuna Wiwaha*, composed by Mpu Kanwa in the reign of King Airlangga around 1035.

This is an allegory of the life of King Airlangga patterned after the *Mahabharata*. Another *kakawin* is the *Bharatayuddha*, begun in 1157, which retells the part of the *Mahabharata* concerning the fight of the five Pandavas with their cousins, the Kuravas. The Javanese version of the *Ramayana* was composed at about the same time. The last great *kakawin*, the *Negarakertagama*, was composed in 1365 when the Majapahit Empire was at its height. It is an indigenous propaganda poem designed to glorify the reign and personality of Hayam Waruk and the Majapahit dynasty. Other indigenous poetic works, such as the romantic *Panji* cycle and a series of historical romances, were written in about the same period.

In the 15th century, with the collapse of the Majapahit Empire, this literary tradition became centred in Java where it continued to prosper. At this time, Islam began to make its appearance and the Javanese language was gradually replaced by Malay in other parts of Western Indonesia. The classical period of Malay literature reached its peak around 1500. Typical of this period are the *Hikayat Hang Tuah*, which tells the story of Hang Tuah, the naval hero, and the *Hikayat Sejarah Melayu* and *Hikayat Aceh*, which are histories of the Malay and Aceh kings. In the post-classical period, many narrative works were written, influenced by Arabic, Persian and Indian works. A particular favourite is the 'Tales of Amir Hamzah' (known as the *Menak* in Java) which relates the extravagantly romantic exploits of a Muslim prince. The 17th century produced the Bugis and Makassar chronicles of contemporary history.

The Balai Pustaka was founded by the Dutch in the early years of the 20th century to encourage Indonesian writing in the Malay language and to translate the great works of European literature into Malay. It published some of the first modern Indonesian novels, such as Mara Roesli's *Siti Nurbaya* and Abdul Muis' *Salah Asuhan*. In 1933 a group of avant-garde writers came together to publish the literary magazine *Pudjangga Baru* ('New Poet'). These writers were concerned with the formation of a national culture to support the growing drive for independence. The extent to which traditional values would have to be usurped by Western ones was a source for debate. Writers such as Takdir Alisjahbana advocated

adopting the Western outlook while others such as Sanusi Pane wished to combine the strength of traditional values with modern concepts of science and technology.

After the Second World War Indonesian writers were very much bound up in the nationalist movement, but anyone wishing to challenge the accepted official line under Sukarno was well advised to keep a very low profile. Today literature is thriving and some of the more famous writers who have won national and international awards are Y. B. Mangun Widjaya, Budidharma and Rendra, who all write commentaries on social and political life in Indonesia. N. H. Dini, Marianne Katoppo and La Rose are all concerned about women's role in Indonesian society and Ike Soepomo is a well known lady novelist.

METALWORK

The use of bronze was introduced into Indonesia with the Dong Son culture from Indo-China after the 7th century BC. The fully fledged tradition of casting is apparent in the cast bronze socketed axes and great kettledrums such as 'The Moon of Bali' found at Pejeng. Bronze and later brass, which is cheaper and easier to use, were cast using the 'lost wax' process to produce marvellous figures of Buddhist and Hindu deities, lamps and ceremonial gongs and bells. This technique is still in use in the Batak and Minangkabau regions of Sumatra. In Java and Bali cast bronze and brass traditional figures are produced in large numbers for the tourist trade.

The gongs and metallophone bars for a *gamelan* are cast using a bronze composed of a ratio of copper to tin of about 10:3. The bronze is cast into slabs which closely resemble the final shape of the bars and into flat sheets for the gongs. The sheets are then beaten on an anvil by up to four hammerers working in perfect co-ordination for the very short time available before the metal must be returned to the fire. This hammering may last for a number of days until finally the hot metal of the fully fashioned gong is quenched in cool water. Tuning of the instrument is accomplished by filing, sandpapering and hammering. It is usually based on the tuning of some well known existing *gamelan* in Java, where there is no absolute pitch or even intervalic structure. The finest Javanese instruments are forged near Surakarta in Central Java and Blahbatuh in Bali.

Iron is rarely used in Indonesia due to the difficulty of working it. Exceptions occur where its hardness is particularly desirable, such as in the making of weapons and the *pinang* scissors needed to crack the hard shell of the *pinang* nut which is chewed with betel leaf and lime in the *sireh* quid. Various weapons are made of iron all over the country but the ceremonial *parang* of the Dayaks of Kalimantan and the *kris* of Java and Bali are particularly important. Both have mystical and ceremonial properties and the smith who makes them enjoys a status and respect by virtue of his craft.

Indonesian gold and silver work has been appreciated for centuries and is used all over the country for household and ceremonial articles of value, such as jewellery and ornaments. Marriages require the bride and, to a lesser extent, the groom to be decked with an assortment of collars, headdresses, rings, earrings, anklets, belts, necklaces and other finery emphasizing the bride's role as queen for the day. If precious metal is too costly, plated or costume jewellery may be substituted or various pieces may be hired for the occasion. Sources of design motifs reflect the cultural influences on Indonesia, from Bronze Age stylized ancestral figures, fertility symbols and spiral decoration through Hindu and Buddhist motifs and the Ottoman and Mogul traditions. Chinese and European designs occur widely.

Precious metals are worked particularly in those areas most influenced by Hinduism. Very fine filigree work in silver is associated with the Minangkabau of West Sumatra and in gold with Aceh. Kendari in South-east Sulawesi is famous for gold and silver filigree jewellery and miniature ships. The metal is wrought to form fine filaments which are drawn through apertures of ever-decreasing diameter and then formed into lacy ornaments, figures and brooches. The small village of Kota Gede outside Yogyakarta, which was once the first capital of the Mataram Kingdom founded in the 16th century, is now famous for its beaten and repoussé silverwork. The village of Kamasan near Klungkung in Bali is a centre for traditional court and temple arts, of which work in gold and silver is an important part. In Nusa Tenggara, itinerant smiths from the island of Ndao traditionally travel the islands making jewellery to order from ingots, scrap metal and old coins.

CARVING

The coastal communities of western Indonesia absorbed much from contact with Chinese and European carving, particularly in furniture design. The great Islamic ceremonial marriage beds of coastal Sumatra, Kalimantan, Sulawesi, Java and Madura show a clear relation to Chinese raised beds. However, the carved *loro blonyo* figures, which are traditionally placed by the bed to bring fertility and prosperity to a Javanese household, are much older. They represent Dewi Sri, fertility and rice goddess, and her consort Sardono. Conversion to Islam and suppression of representation of the human form has resulted in the use of geometrical designs of great vitality carved on doorways and internal walls in coastal houses.

In Bali the integration of art, religion and everyday life became nearly complete. Wood and stone carving was used on public buildings, temples and palaces as an adjunct to architecture, while free-standing statues served as protective figures or representations of divinities. Domestic architecture was generally simple, with carving only found at the gate and around the family temple. In a palace, however, Hindu deities might be sited on a main cross beam, lion figures would be placed on each side of a door and figures of flying mermaids and demons would have their place.

The use of soft, grey volcanic tuff, wood and cloth meant that carvers were kept busy renewing the decorations on palaces and public buildings. When patronage from the palaces declined, as the palaces themselves declined, carvers had to look to foreign visitors to buy their work and they adapted it accordingly. Thus carving revolutionized itself in the 1930s just as painting was doing at the same time, though without the direct stimulus of European influence. The carvers experimented with new subjects and more refined sculptural lines. Instead of painting and gilding, they began to use the plain polished wood grain as surface decoration. A highly stylized, elongated school, reminiscent of the work of Alberto Giacometti, grew up. Ida Bagus Nyana and his son Ida Bagus Tilem of Mas created startling abstract carvings in this elongated style and also in a more rounded, reposeful style. Both command high prices on the international market.

Other styles were originated and much copied, as had always been the case in Bali. Ngurah Umum of Gianyar created the colourful wooden ducks to be found everywhere and Nyoman Togog of Peliatan the carved miniature trees and tropical fruit. Wooden models of frogs driving aeroplanes or Volkswagens, tourists carrying cameras, plates and non-traditional masks are now all common and of widely variable quality.

Batak, Minangkabau and Toraja houses are carved with geometrical and representational figures coloured with natural dyes, while their furniture is traditionally simple stools and worktables, often totally undecorated. The people of Nias Island copy their outdoor stone furniture in wood for use indoors. The ancestor sculptures of these tribes are unusual for their stylized head-dresses, small beards and a distended right ear lobe. The great Batak chests are carved with the *singa* or lion head and their magic staffs bear an entwined relief of figures and other motifs struggling to the top of the stout hardwood pole, on the top of which is carved a free-standing figure of a head. Both the Batak and the Toraja make very clean-lined and simple ritual dishes and utensils from a single piece of hardwood with carved handles.

Dayak carving relies heavily on Chinese motifs, even if these have become highly stylized in the borrowing. Typical examples can be seen on wooden baby-carriers carved with a protective motif frieze, sickness figures which are floated away on the river to carry away illness, and the tall poles representing ancestors. Figures of humans and animals keep guard over the fields and small wooden figures are placed strategically around the village to confuse the spirits of disease and ill fortune; tiny charm figures bring good luck. The superb deer horn handles of the Dayak *mandau* or ceremonial *parang* are carved with human, animal and plant motifs and decorated with hair and beadwork.

The Asmat people of the southern coastal swamps of Irian Jaya are master carvers. Their tradition of dramatic carving has always been symbolically linked to the continuous

tribal warfare which was a feature of the area. The government's desire to stamp out this warfare, and the cannibalism and head-hunting which went with it, resulted in the early 1960s in the prohibition of the celebration of the warrior cult in carving. This completely disorientated the cultural life of the Asmat. Attempts are now being made by the government, and certain Catholic groups, to reintroduce traditional carving at co-operative ventures. The large memorial poles, up to 8 metres (26 feet) high, carved with figures and the animals and birds of the Asmat spirit world, are again being produced. Canoe paddles and openwork canoe prows are again being made. In addition, the Asmat produce a variety of shields, plaques, drums and sago bowls from hardwood and the sacred mangrove. The wood is polished with shells and stained with charcoal, lime and a red earth dye. Whether the standard of carving

will remain as high as before, now that its main inspiration has been removed, only time will tell.

TEXTILES

Indonesia produces an enormous range of textiles which are seen all over the country as an adjunct of everyday life as well as at times of ceremony. They are made in a variety of ways which vary from region to region but, though certain of the techniques are found in geographically widely separated areas, common themes can be detected throughout.

Origins

The technique of weaving originated in China and was brought to Indonesia some time around the beginning of the first millennium BC. As the trade routes with Arabia opened up, further skills were acquired from India via the Indonesian trading posts

Bugis women weaving at Balikpapan, Kalimantan, 1906. The fine ikat *cloth that has been produced by these people, and others, for centuries, is justly famous for its intricate designs and bold colours.*

such as the Srivijaya capital of Palembang. Textiles are mentioned in the gift lists which accompany the stone or copper *Sima* charters from Java as early as the 9th century. By the 11th century textiles were being traded in the Javanese five-day markets and silk was being produced locally. By the 13th century Bali, Java and Sumatra were exporting textiles to China.

Materials

Indonesian textiles use both locally available and imported materials. Cotton has long been grown as a side crop on the rice fields at the end of the wet season, when it receives the moisture it requires during its growing period and later benefits from the dry conditions needed at maturity. There has been a silk industry in Sumatra from the time of the Srivijayan Empire and it has flourished on and off ever since, though now most indigenous silk is produced in Sulawesi. Neither the moths which produce silk nor the mulberry trees on which they feed are native to Indonesia and early silk was imported, typically from China. Many other fibres are employed in Indonesia, including the pineapple leaf fibre of the Iban and Kayan peoples of Kalimantan and the palm leaf fibre of the Toraja people. Gold and silver thread, which was once made in Indonesia, is now mostly imported from Europe, India and Japan. The use of felted bark as barkcloth, common in the Pacific, is also found. Synthetic fabrics are, of course, now used widely everywhere.

Dyes

We know that Indonesia has been producing natural dyes for a thousand years and, although most textile factories today use industrial dyes, there are still small producers who dye cloth using only natural products. Dyeing is a very complex business as some substances cannot be used directly but require a mordant or, as in Bali, mixing with coconut oil, and they may be more suitable for one fabric than for another. Some traditional colours are blue-black from the indigo plant, red, brown and purple from the Sappan tree or the Betel palm and yellow from turmeric or from the Safflower, which was known in ancient Egypt and was introduced into Indonesia via India. The Iban and Dusun of Kalimantan use the covering of the fruit of the Dragon's Blood Rattan and the red chilli pepper is used as a dye in northern Kalimantan.

Tie Dyeing

The resist-dye method, in which areas of yarn or cloth not meant to take the dye are tied off or coated, is common.

Ikat is the most widely distributed of these techniques. For this, the yarns are tied in bundles before dyeing, with the binding forming the resist material. The smaller the bundle the higher the quality. Warp *ikat*, where the warp only is dyed, is found in Batak Sumatra, in Toraja Sulawesi, among the Iban people and in Eastern Indonesia. It is usually woven on a continuous warp. Weft *ikat* was introduced from India and is mostly found in those areas with international trading connections, often being used in court circles. Fine weft *ikat* is found in South Sumatra and Bali and is also produced by the Bugis and the Makassarese of Sulawesi as well as in East Java, Lombok and Riau.

Double *ikat*, where both the warp and the weft are bundled and dyed, is found only in the village of Tenganan in Bali. The process is a very delicate and difficult one, as the yarns must be stretched on separate frames and constantly checked for alignment against each other and against a pattern. Double *ikat* is tubular when removed from the loom. In this form it is used to clothe deities; once cut it may be worn only by humans. It is thought to have protective powers and is commonly used ritually.

The technique of single dyed warp and weft produces a vast variety of striped and checked cloth from all over Indonesia, some of the finest being the checked silk of Ujung Pandang. Other tie-dyeing processes are *pelangi* from Sulawesi, where complete sections of cloth are tied to produce patterns after they are dyed, and *teritik* from Central Java where the designs are stitched onto the cloth before dyeing and then cut away afterwards to reveal the pattern.

Batik

Batik textiles are among the most beautiful produced in Indonesia and are probably the best known. The process, which uses wax as a dye-resist, is generally associated with Indonesia and Malaysia, but the technique has been known in Egypt since the 5th or 6th centuries AD, and is also found in Africa, China, Japan and Central Asia. It has been suggested that intricate batik design is relatively modern, but the examples collected by Sir Stamford Raffles while he was Governor of Java in the early years of the 19th century already show a well-established tradition.

The finest batik uses cloth with a high thread density and a flat, even surface. Such cloth was imported from Europe and India, and is now bought from Japan as well. Once cut to length, hemmed, washed and boiled to remove the size, it is oiled and treated with a rice paste to prevent the wax penetrating too deeply. For the best, hand-painted batik, known as *tulis*, the wax is applied to the areas to resist the first dyeing, using a small spouted pot called a *canting*. The cloth is dipped in the dye and then into cold water to harden the wax so that it may be scraped off. More wax is then applied to further areas and the process repeated until the pattern is complete. Good batik has the wax patterns repeated on the back of the fabric so that it is reversible. Cracks in the wax, intended or not, give the familiar spidery background patterns. A 2 metre (6 foot) length of the best-quality batik can take up to two months to complete. Batik *tulis*, with fine quality, hand-painted designs, is traditionally made by women, often the wives of high officials. Batik *cap* is a more economical method using a metal stamp to apply the wax pattern to the cloth, and is traditionally a male preserve.

Java is the home of batik, which is seen at its best in the courts of Yogyakarta and Surakarta. An imprecise way of telling the difference is the use in Yogyakarta of browns and blues against a white background whereas in Surakarta the background is yellow. South Sumatra and the Toraja region of Sulawesi also produce good batik.

Motifs

Some of the motifs found today on Indonesian textiles are thought to have very early origins. The angular and maze-like patterns traditional in Sumatra and central Kalimantan may derive from the geometric designs found on the great bronze drums of the Dong Son period, some two thousand years ago. The frontal stylized human figure found on cloths of Flores, Lembata and Sumba in Nusa Tenggara, Kisar and Tanimbar in Maluku, and in Timor, resembles some of the Iban designs of Kalimantan and can be detected in the ship cloths of Sumatra. It is thought to be a very ancient motif partly because it is presumed to be an ancestor figure and partly because of its association with one of the earliest weaving techniques, the warp *ikat*.

The *tumpal* border, which is essentially a series of triangles, is another very ancient motif found on early bronze drums and on imported Indian fabrics. Today it is common on the Malay Peninsula as a border for *songket* weaving and in Borneo, South Sulawesi and Sumbawa, as well as being used as a border on Javanese batik.

Chinese derived motifs are also found. The most obvious are probably the *megamendung* batiks of Cirebon on the north coast of Java, with their swirling cloud designs in various shades of blue. The lattice pattern designs on classical Javanese batik may also be based on Chinese designs. More modern foreign derived motifs can be traced to European sources, such as ships, coats of arms and cannon. More recently still, cars, helicopters and bicycles have made their appearance. Some common motifs found in widely separated regions may simply have arisen spontaneously from the processes of weaving and dyeing: triangle, diamond and zig-zag patterns are examples.

The richest of the Indonesian fabric traditions, that of Javanese batik, contains over 3,000 discernible patterns of which some are indigenous and some seem to be foreign. They may be categorized under four main headings: *isen*, or background designs; geometric designs; *semen*, or non-geometric designs; and proscribed designs. *Isen* designs consist of a series of small repeated circles or semi-circles, often looking rather like coffee beans. Geometric patterns can include highly stylized flowers, fruits and animals. Among the most famous of these are the *garis miring* diagonal scroll designs such as the *parang*. Some of these patterns could traditionally be worn only by royalty. The *semen* or non-geometrical designs include botanical motifs, birds such as the garuda, phoenix, peacock and cockerel, and animals, both real and mythological.

Decorative Techniques

Many ways of decorating cloth have been handed down through the generations. Beadwork, for example, is used to decorate textiles in many parts of Indonesia, notably Sumatra, Sulawesi and Flores and by the Dayak peoples of Kalimantan. The Balinese have developed great expertise in painting cloth. Usually the polychromatic cloths still found in Bali depict scenes from Indian Hindu literature, received through Java, and Balinese calendars which record auspicious days. Gold, in the form of leaf, paint and dust, is also used.

OTHER CRAFTS
Basketwork

The art of basketry has long been practised throughout Indonesia and there is a vast supply of fibres suitable for plaiting into containers, mats, hats, screens and many other household and decorative items. The strongest is unsplit rattan which is used for such things as the framework for furniture and for the baskets in which pigs are traditionally carried to market. When split it can be plaited more easily and, when very finely split, can produce a material as soft and flexible as a coarse cotton. Leaves of the *Pandanus* tree are much softer and easier to work but are less durable and tend to be used for articles which get light wear or for mats which can easily be replaced. Palm leaf is ingeniously and widely used in Bali for little baskets for offerings and an amazing variety of decorations for temple ceremonies. Other fibres and grasses are used where they are abundantly available.

Probably the most interesting plaited ware is found among the tribes of Kalimantan. The Penan are considered the best plaiters and mat makers but the Kayan and Kenyah peoples also produce very fine work. The best of Penan work, plaited from split rattan, is reputed to be both water- and insect-proof. Plaited rattan is used in Kalimantan for many purposes, from war shields to baskets and screens. Decorative motifs are obtained by the insertion of dyed or stained strips of different colours. These are very varied and include rhomb, key and spiral motifs with stylized human or spirit figures, animals and birds often used in horizontal bands. Baskets and mats are always plaited diagonally and some mats have the decoration plaited into the fabric so that it can be seen only when held obliquely to the light.

The *ingan* basket, made principally by the Kayans but found in various forms throughout Kalimantan, is typical. It is reinforced by four sticks which protrude a few centimetres below the base to form four feet, while the lip is strengthened with bamboo to keep its circular shape. Sometimes as tall as a metre (3 feet), the *ingan* is used in the longhouse for storing rice and personal possessions. Fitted with bark or rattan shoulder-straps it can be used to carry large loads over long distances. A very finely plaited form of this basket, lined with

skin or bark and with a well-fitting lid, was formerly used to store human heads before they were hung in the longhouse.

Beadwork

Natural objects such as stones and seeds have always been popular as decoration on clothing and artefacts. When small highly coloured glass beads were first imported in the 15th century from Venice, they immediately became very sought-after throughout South-east Asia. The Dayak peoples started using them early on in intricate designs on almost all forms of art and craft. Motifs include both geometrical patterns and all manner of anthropomorphs, animals, birds, spiders and plants. Traditionally the patterns were created in black and yellow, or white and dark blue with, occasionally, the addition of red. Rarely were all the colours used on the same article, though this is now common. In addition to the small glass beads the status of a person in the longhouse may be demonstrated by the wearing of large beads made into skull caps, necklaces and collars.

Among both the Toraja and Batak peoples glass beads are also revered as possessing magical properties. Long strings of beads are worn only by Batak princes and the masked celebrants at princely funerals. In Toraja, beads and brightly coloured little cylinders are made into necklaces and other ornaments for women and into girdles and neck collars to be worn at special ceremonies.

In Timor, where glass beads are not common, dyed seeds are used to make bright coverings for betel-nut containers and other articles. The colours are traditionally red, blue, black and yellow.

Ceramics

Pottery and ceramics have never been widespread crafts in Indonesia because of the abundance of fibre substitutes and materials such as coconut shell and bamboo for use as containers. Also, ceramics were imported from China in massive quantities as early as the 8th century. Some pieces gained religious importance, such as the great dragon jars up to 1.5 metres (5 feet) tall so much prized by the Dayaks.

Some pottery is made throughout the islands, often without the use of the potter's wheel, but it is generally fairly basic. The *kendi* or water pitcher is found all over the country. It comes in various styles but is essentially an unglazed container with a spout designed to be held away from the drinker's lips as the water is poured. Evaporation through the unglazed sides lowers the temperature of the contents. Terracotta votive statues and groups are made in Java, Bali, Sulawesi and eastern Indonesia, while terracotta tiles and roof finials are made in East Java and Bali.

INDONESIA TODAY

AGRICULTURE
Agriculture is the most important sector of the Indonesian economy, since the vast majority of Indonesians depend on it either directly or indirectly. Its importance as a proportion of the country's gross domestic product (GDP) is, however, declining.

Rice
Within the agricultural sector, rice is the most important commodity as it forms the staple diet of most Indonesians and is gaining ground even in those areas where other staples such as corn, cassava or sago are traditionally used. Intensive, irrigated rice cultivation is mostly found on Java, Madura and Bali. However, dry rice is grown throughout the archipelago and new areas of intensive irrigation are being brought into production outside the traditional areas. By 1984-5 increased yields resulting from improved strains of plant, better pest control and better management had enabled Indonesia, formerly a major rice importer, to achieve self-sufficiency. Production by 2005 was expected to reach 53 million tonnes.

Plantations
The plantation industry in Indonesia is huge, with over 11 million hectares (27 million acres) in total, of which only about 10 per cent are state-owned enterprises. The traditional crops are rubber and oil palm (of which Indonesia is the world's largest producer), coffee, tea, sugar, cocoa, tobacco and pepper. Cloves have a very large domestic market due to their use in the typical Indonesian cigarette, the *kretek*, which is smoked by the million every day and contains up to 60 per cent clove. So great is the consumption of cloves for this

purpose that Indonesia, which once supplied cloves to the world, is now a net importer.

Plantations were started by the Dutch and have generally been foreign-owned until recently. The original principle was to cultivate and harvest a centrally managed area with waged labour. The area would serve a central mill or factory and the produce would be exported via a company-owned port facility. The scale of the operation required very large funds to establish the plantation and maintain it from planting to maturity and, later, to finance the unproductive period during which the trees have to be grubbed out and replaced. The central installation, particularly in the case of oil palm and sugar, is a major engineering work.

Recently the trend has been towards production areas centred on a nucleus estate that is surrounded by many small-holdings. Each family works its own area but is helped in cultivation, finance and quality control by a central management which buys the produce, maintains the facilities and looks after marketing. This is happening on established plantations and especially in the new areas which are being cleared in the outer islands and settled by families from the over-populated regions under the *transmigrasi* scheme.

Fisheries
The seas around Indonesia are very rich in fish, always a very important part of the local diet. Large-scale commercial sea fishing has been very much in the hands of the big international companies, based not in Indonesia but in their home countries. The recent granting of archipelagic status should help the government to control this activity and to develop the potential for exploitation by Indonesia. Inland fish-farming is another area of potential which is already being exploited, particularly in the production of freshwater prawns for the Japanese market. Another small but growing market is that for tropical fish for private aquaria.

Forests
Indonesia still has about 10 per cent of the world's rainforest cover but unsupervised and uncontrolled logging in the 1960s and 1970s has put much of the forest at risk. Efforts are being made to control logging

and to limit the plywood industry and the export of whole logs to Japan. A policy of designating areas as 'protection forest', which is left totally undisturbed, 'park and reserve forest', with provides for tourism, and 'production forest', which is exploited on a sustainable basis, should go a long way towards improving the situation.

Other forest products such as rattan and the illipe nut are important commodities. Some jungle plants, such as orchids, can be successfully cultivated. The market in the West for orchids as cut flowers is large and profitable, provided the logistics of getting plant to customer in the shortest time can be mastered. Indonesia has so far had only a small share of this market but it could grow. The market for rare orchids is a completely different one and involves the collecting and hybridizing of very high value plants, most of which are destined for orchid fanciers in the region who are prepared to pay enormous prices for unusual specimens.

MINERALS
Oil and Gas
Pertamina is the state oil and gas company responsible for managing all Indonesia's oil, gas and geothermal energy industries. Its activities cover exploration, production, refining, marketing and supply for both foreign and domestic markets. It is also developing a national petro-chemical industry. Pertamina is the world's largest producer of liquefied natural gas from two sources, the Arun field off the coast of North Sumatra and its onshore processing plant, and the Bontang field in East Kalimantan.

The presence of oil deposits in North Sumatra had been known since the 1860s. A Dutch company, usually known as 'de Koninklijke', was set up in 1883 and test drilling began, but production did not start until 1892. In 1901 the same company expanded into Kalimantan. In 1897 the Shell Transport and Trading Company was set up in London with British capital to undertake exploration in East Kalimantan and merged with de Koninklijke in 1907 to form Royal Dutch Shell. By 1930 Shell was producing about 85 per cent of Indonesia's oil and American and Japanese companies were taking up major concessions. Today

Indonesia is both an exporter and an importer of crude oil since her low-sulphur oil commands a higher price on the world markets than Middle East crude. In 1999 oil, gas and minerals accounted for about 20 per cent of total exports.

Tin

Tin has been mined in Indonesia since the 17th century. Its main source is on Bangka Island, part of the 'Tin Belt' which runs down the western side of the mountain ranges of southern Thailand and Peninsular Malaysia, down the east coast of Sumatra through the Singkep and Bangka Islands and across via the island of Belitung to the western part of Kalimantan.

Tin is found in the overburden of jagged limestone and is mined by various methods, the most basic of which uses shovels and panning in much the same way as in the days of the American gold rush. Modern mines use large mechanized dredges capable of shifting vast volumes of material, leaving behind them 'tin-tailings' of muddy sludge which are difficult to develop usefully. High-pressure water-hose extraction is another method. The metal is smelted in the state company's smelter on Bangka and exported in ingots or as anode tin or tin shot. Principle uses are for tin plate and for alloying with other metals. The big tourist market for pewter, an alloy of tin and lead, has not been exploited in Indonesia as it has in Malaysia and Singapore.

Coal

Large deposits of coal have been known for centuries in Sumatra and Kalimantan. Until comparatively recently, little use has been made of them but now large-scale plans are being realized to exploit these easily

Tobacco plantation in Sumatra, 1899. Today, instead of being large centrally managed areas as they were in the past, plantations tend to be worked as a series of family smallholdings.

extracted deposits by open-cast mining. Indonesian coal has the disadvantages of low calorific value and high moisture content, and the advantages of low sulphur and ash content which result in lower pollution when burnt. Coal production reached 132 million metric tons in 2004.

Other Minerals

Copper, gold and silver are found in the same deposits and the most successful company to exploit these minerals to date is PT Freeport which is operating in the Fakfak Regency of Irian Jaya. Other companies are prospecting in Irian Jaya and in Sulawesi, Aceh and South Lampung. Bauxite is found in much the same areas as tin and is mostly exported, for lack of local facilities, to be turned into alumina suitable to act as feedstock for the largely Japanese-owned aluminium smelter on the east coast of Sumatra. Nickel and manganese are also potentially important.

INDUSTRY
Electricity
The supply of electricity in a country as large and fragmented as Indonesia has always been a considerable problem and has become more critical with the increased expectations of the population and the needs of industry. Major efforts have been made to increase the generating capacity and to develop the high-tension power networks required to distribute electricity. There is a move away from oil-fired power stations towards natural gas and hydro-electricity. The recently appreciated coal resource is also expected to be used for stations coming on stream in the future.

Although Indonesia is among a handful of countries to develop geothermal energy, utilization of geothermal potential has proceeded very slowly and faces difficult challenges and uncertainty. Solar energy has an obvious attraction for a country with such a high level of sunshine and it may be that its use will be viable in the future, particularly in remote areas. At the moment the cost of solar energy production is far higher than generated electricity or diesel-generated power for such things as rural water pumps. A major rural electrification programme has been under way for the past 40 years.

Industry
The Agency for Strategic Industries (BPIS), presided over by the Minister of State for Research and Technology, comprises ten high-tech industries, ranging from steel-making to telecommunications, designed to accelerate Indonesia's advance into the ranks of the developed countries. The most important and, some would say, the most costly venture is IPTN, the Indonesian Aircraft Industry. Another huge part of the Agency for Strategic Industries is the Surabaya-based PAL Indonesia, which is a major shipbuilder with capacity to construct tankers, bulk carriers and container vessels up to 50,000 tonnes. It is also active in the military and maintenance and overhaul sectors.

Major industries operate in all sectors of the Indonesian economy, with or without overt links to the army or government. Cars are assembled locally with foreign partners. Cement is another important industry. Export industries include textiles and the manufacture of shoes and garments for owners of internationally known brand names. The manufacture of plain and decorative plywood and veneer is a big export revenue earner. Small-scale industries producing handicrafts making use of natural products such as rattan, which used to be exported unworked, are being encouraged through local co-operatives. The export value of leather and garments produced by small-scale industries has recently exceeded that of crafts and general products.

COMMUNICATIONS
Road communications in Indonesia are being expanded and improved all the time and a number of toll roads are being built by private enterprise. Facilities such as coach stations have been modernized and public transport is being upgraded in urban areas with trailer buses and air-conditioned buses. Efforts are also being made in the big cities to alleviate traffic congestion. Railways exist only in Java and Sumatra, but the services that are there are being improved by the introduction of modern rolling-stock and dedicated commuter and tourist trains. A faster freight service has been introduced between Jakarta and Surabaya with a container transportation system.

The number and comfort of both local and inter-island ferries have been greatly improved, particularly in Nusa Tenggara. Local ferries run regularly depending on demand and there are also inter-island and coastal shipping services run by the state shipping line, Pelni. These ships run round trips calling at a number of ports to a published timetable. In addition, there are traditional craft from the elegant Bugis schooners to very dodgy passenger and cargo ships which sail at unscheduled times to no definite itinerary. In Kalimantan the rivers have always been the lines of communication and even today are very important. Ferry services run up and down all the major rivers linking the settlements on their banks.

Air travel in Indonesia is indispensable. The number of islands and the distances on or between them make flying the only efficient means of long-distance transport. Although few airports are capable of taking the larger passenger aircraft there are a lot of smaller airports in even the most remote areas. These are served by a collection of airlines flying a large number of different types of aircraft. In Irian Jaya, for instance, the terrain is such that only light aircraft can operate out of the highland strips.

Postal services cover the whole of the country and are steadily being upgraded. Mobile post offices serve the smaller villages. The telecommunications network took a turn for the better with the commissioning in 1992 of Indonesia's three satellite systems based on its Palapa satellites.

TOURISM
Tourism is a rapidly growing industry in Indonesia. The number of foreign visitors in 2001 reached 5 million, bringing in US$5.43 million. Holiday-makers now arrive from all over the world, the majority from Australia and Japan, while regional tourism from countries such as Singapore and Malaysia is ever increasing.

Bali was already a tourist destination in the 1930s, but the Second World War and the subsequent period of instability reduced the number of visitors to a trickle. By 1970 tourism was again big business in Bali and has expanded exponentially. New resorts were opened indiscriminately and, although the excesses of Pattaya Beach in Thailand were avoided, many thought that the island's ambience would be destroyed. Swift action by the government and the resilience of the Balinese people has stopped this happening.

Other traditional tourist areas, like Central Java with its world-famous monuments of Borobudur and Prambanan, and the courtly and cultural life of Yogyakarta, have coped well with the influx. The Lake Toba area of North Sumatra was a popular weekend destination before the war for visitors from Penang and is so again, with additional travellers from Singapore availing themselves of the direct flights to Medan now offered by the regional airlines.

A new development of recent years is eco-tourism. This is based on concern for the environment and the perilous position of a number of the most famous animals of the region. As national parks and reserves have been established, the few scientists working in them have been greatly outnumbered by tourist arrivals. For some, the spectacular landscape and physical features, such as the volcanoes and mountains of Java and Sumatra, are the draw. For others the chance to make a safe, guided expedition into the jungle with, perhaps, a glimpse of a tiger, elephants or a rhinoceros, comes once in a lifetime. However, unlike the safari parks of East Africa, tropical forest does not permit prolonged close encounters with the larger animals. Only in Komodo, where the famous Komodo Dragon can be approached and photographed in the wild, does anything similar occur. For this reason the Orang-utan rehabilitation centres are popular because they offer a rare chance to see semi-wild apes close up. The income that tourists bring to the reserves can be ploughed back into conservation and research.

The government is encouraging the development of tourism on the outer islands, with the provision of hotels and tourist facilities. Sulawesi and the islands of eastern Indonesia are all now holiday destinations. New activities are being exploited, such as diving off the magnificent coral reefs of Kalimantan, Sulawesi, Nusa Tenggara and Maluku, where brilliant displays of tropical fish and wide, unspoilt beaches are additional attractions. Caves in Aceh and South Sulawesi provide an idea of how humans and animals lived 30,000 years ago and are the habitat of rare bats and birds. White-water rafting is becoming popular on some of the less tranquil rivers in the national parks.

Some of the islands in eastern Indonesia are totally unspoilt and possess stunning scenery, beautiful beaches and crumbling monuments to the past importance of the spice trade. The government is anxious that the advent of tourism should not ruin these small havens and seeks to control the style and level of development. Indeed, it is to be hoped that increasingly easy access will be regulated by a sensitive exploitation of Indonesia's natural and irreplaceable beauty.

INDONESIA TOMORROW

Indonesia is a very rich country with a very large population. It has all the requirements for accelerated growth in the years to come if no obstacles arise.

Political stability is a problem following the long reign of Suharto and the succession of presidents since. However, the election of the president and vice-president by universal suffrage in 2004 augurs well for future political stability. The newly-won open society and the hitherto unknown freedom of the press offer an optimistic future. The separatist tendencies in parts of this far-flung archipelago, such as in Aceh and Irian Jaya/West Papua, are also a source of concern, as is the rise of Islamic fundamentalism, though this does not appear a serious threat at the moment. Another problem is how to tackle the huge number of young people who come onto the job market every year.

Given political stability, there is no reason why the technology which is already in place should not blossom, as skills are learnt and the population becomes more wealthy – 215 million people form a marvellous domestic market, if they have any disposable income. Improved communications, radio and television will help to bind the nation together, although greater exposure to Western values through satellite, video and cinema may lead to increased expectations and a breakdown of traditional values, particularly in rural areas.

Indonesia is already becoming the dominant power in South-east Asia and this position is likely to be consolidated. It is 60 years since the declaration of independence on 17 August 1945. Much has been achieved in that time and much more will be achieved in the next 60 years.

THE LAND

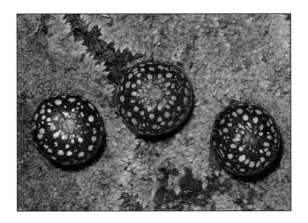

Indonesia is a gigantic archipelago stretching from Burma in a vast arc to the northern tip of Australia. It consists of some 13,700 islands including five of the ten largest islands in the world. It lies at the meeting-point of four of the tectonic plates of the earth's crust, whose relative movements have thrown up a line of volcanoes forming a spine of high mountains. Java and Bali, with their fertile rice-growing land, are home to the greater part of Indonesia's population of 190 million. Other parts of the country, such as Irian Jaya and Kalimantan, are much less densely populated.

Sumatra and Kalimantan are still covered with tropical rainforest in spite of continued logging. National parks and reserves have been established and attempts are being made to reverse the decline in endangered species. Sumatra and Kalimantan have some of the highest rainfalls in the world, swelling the great rivers whose sediment has formed the coastal swamps. Further east, the rainfall becomes more seasonal and a pronounced dry season dominates the year. The islands provide beautiful and unspoilt beaches, clear water, coral and exotic tropical fish.

Indonesia has great natural wealth. The state oil and gas company is the world's largest producer of liquefied natural gas. Tin production is among the largest in the world; coal potential enormous. Copper is mined in Irian Jaya and gold, silver, nickel, manganese and bauxite are important exports. Indonesia is the world's largest producer of rubber and palm oil and a major producer of coffee, tea, sugar, cocoa, tobacco, cloves, nutmeg and pepper. The forests provide timber, rattan and various plants which are only now being researched as sources of medicine or new cultivars for commercial agriculture. The seas are rich in fish which provide the main source of protein for much of the population.

Above: *Lake Toba in North Sumatra, the largest crater lake in the world, was formed by a series of prehistoric volcanic eruptions.*
Opposite: *The Alas River, still used as one of Sumatra's main highways, flows through the Mount Leuser National Park. The dipterocarp forest stretching away from its banks contains a great diversity of plant species, including* (right) *colourful wild gingers.*

PREVIOUS PAGES
Page 52: *Indonesia is a country of mountains and water. The craters of extinct volcanoes contain cool, high lakes such as Maninjau in West Sumatra* (above left) *and the dramatic crater lake of the Ijen volcano in East Java* (below left). *By contrast, the mountains of Tanah Toraja in Central Sulawesi* (below right) *are not volcanic but the result of tectonic movements. Beautiful lakes abound in Kalimantan, Sumatra, Sulawesi and Irian Jaya, such as Lake Sentani near Jayapura* (above right).
Page 53: *Fruits of the Creeping Fig* (Ficus aurantiaca).

In the Minangkabau region of West Sumatra irrigated rice is the staple crop. The traditional roofs with their upswept eaves rising to tall pinnacles can be seen above the banana plants in this village near Bukittinggi (above). Mount Merapi in the background is an active volcano from whose top a wisp of smoke escapes. In another village in the area (opposite) a group of humbler houses are roofed with corrugated metal. The mosque with its onion dome is the grandest building.

Left: Mount Kerinci (3,800 metres; 12,500 feet), in the Kerinci-Seblat National Park in western Sumatra, is the highest mountain in Indonesia outside Irian Jaya and is a still-active volcano. Its upper slopes are bare because of frequent coverings of hot ash and sulphur-laden air.

Above: *Although Indonesia's tropical rainforest is endangered by insensitive logging, much remains. The Kerinci-Seblat National Park in West Sumatra is one of the largest undisturbed areas of dipterocarp forest. Here, the trees grow to a height of more than 50 metres (165 feet) and a host of other plants struggle for light under the dense canopy. In the forest depths are found all the major animals of Sumatra except the Orang-utan.*

Left: *A view from about 3,300 metres (11,000 feet) on Mount Kerinci. The montane forest in the foreground gives way to lowland rainforest and then to land cleared for agricultural use.*

Above: *When the volcano of Krakatau erupted in 1883 the group of small islands which takes its name was smothered in debris and the land sterilized. A new island, Anak Krakatau ('Son of Krakatau'), emerged from the sea only in 1930. It has been possible to study the colonization of a virgin site by plants imported by wind or birds. The coast has been colonized by the She-oak* (Casuarina equisetifolia) *and wild sugarcane, grasses and ferns are appearing further inland.*

Left: Phaius flavus *is a large terrestrial orchid found extensively in South-east Asia, while (far left) the rare* Paphiopedilum victoria-mariae *is found only in Sumatra and is much prized by orchid collectors.*

The craters of dormant or active volcanoes such as Mount Gede in West Java (left) *may look as though nothing except thorns would be tough enough to survive there. However, plants such as the Javanese Edelweiss* (Anaphalis javanica) *are found* (below left) *flowering amid the sulphurous fumes on the crater lip. Below the summit but still at around 3,000 metres (10,000 feet), tree ferns thrive, showing their delicate tracery against the sky* (below) .

Opposite: *Rice paddies are planted and harvested year round in the lush rural landscape of West Java, near Mount Halimun. Amidst the greenery, the huge leaves of banana plants are instantly recognizable. The tumbling river is crossed by a bamboo bridge.*

Above: *The East Javan coast near Meru Betiri National Park, where the forests reach down to the sea, and flowering plants such as this Hibiscus species (left) can be found.*

Opposite: *The volcanic complex of the ancient caldera of Tengger in East Java contains the comparatively recent volcanoes of Bromo, Batok and Kursi. It is one of the great volcanic sites of the world. This stunning view from the lip of the caldera includes the active Semeru volcano in the rear. 'Bromo' is the Javanese pronunciation of 'Brahma' and this mountain was worshipped during the Hindu Majapahit period as a holy mountain and the seat of the gods.*

Above: *These sculptured rice terraces at Tirtagangga in southern Bali show the complexity of the organization required to ensure equitable water distribution.*

Left: *Across the Lombok Straits from Bali lies Lombok Island in Nusa Tenggara. Here it is seen from Gili Meno, one of three tiny islands off its north-west coast.*

Opposite: *Mount Batur, a dormant volcano in Central Bali, towers over Lake Batur, which fills part of the caldera of an ancient volcano.*

Right: *An aerial view of the wild and rugged Rakit Island in Teluk Saleh, an almost landlocked bay on the island of Sumbawa in Nusa Tenggara.*

Opposite: *Rising out of the crater lake of Mount Rinjani in Lombok is a new volcanic cone, only a couple of hundred years old. At 3,726 metres (12,224 feet), Mount Rinjani is Indonesia's third highest mountain. The hot sulphur springs at the base of the main crater (below) are considered to have therapeutic properties, which may be needed after the three-day ascent of the mountain.*

Abo
the r

Righ
of th
the b
the t
eartl

Above: *The scenic west coast of Lombok, where the main resort, Senggigi Beach, overlooks the Lombok Straits. Drier, more rugged and, as yet, less commercialized than neighbouring Bali, Lombok has a charm and character of its own.*

Opp
all th
Kom
Islan
back
wate
trea
Islan

The lowland rainforest around Samarinda, the capital of East Kalimantan, has often been overlogged, as gaps in the forest canopy indicate (opposite above), *but it is still home to an astonishing variety of flora and fauna, including many species of ginger* (opposite below right) *and fungi which play an essential part in the food chain of the tropical rainforest* (right and opposite below left). *The Ohong River* (above) *leads off Lake Jampang, part of the Mahakam River system which flows through the area around Samarinda. River systems like this often provide the only efficient means of transport through the lowland rainforest.*

Left: *This rainforest by the Sangatta River in the Kutai National Park, East Kalimantan, has been logged but will regenerate naturally if left undisturbed. The relogging cycle is something of the order of 80 years, depending on size control and extraction damage.*

Below left: *The attractive but invasive Water Hyacinth (Eichornia crassipes) is a scourge of inland waterways as its fleshy stalks spread rapidly, causing blockages.*

Below right: *A wild arrowroot,* Tacca integrifolia, *growing in Kutai National Park.*

Peat produces the black water of the Sekunir River in Tanjung Puting National Park, Central Kalimantan (above). Here, near the Camp Leakey Research Station, Screwpine (Pandanus) and Hanguana malayana dominate the forest fringe. The peat swamps are generally above the level of the surrounding land so that they form an acid, undecomposed closed environment where only certain plants can survive, such as (right) the orchid Vanda hookeriana. This is often found in sunny spots in peat swamps where it is able to take up the nutrients it needs from rain and does not have to rely on the acid swamp itself.

Above: *In Tanah Toraja, Central Sulawesi, this village has grown up on the banks of a river where the flat valley bottom can be used for irrigated rice with a minimum of terracing. The river provides the route by which any surplus rice can be exported and other commodities imported.*

Left: *The Bantimurung Park, some 45 kilometres (28 miles) outside Ujung Pandang in South Sulawesi, has caves and a number of spectacular waterfalls which are very popular with the residents of Ujung Pandang at weekends and holidays.*

Above: *Irrigated rice fields in Central Sulawesi: the small buildings are erected for the watchmen who guard the fields as harvest-time approaches against seed-eating munia birds, which might otherwise devour the entire crop.*

Right: *This village on the shores of Lake Poso in Central Sulawesi has little flat land nearby on which to grow rice. Instead the inhabitants rely on fishing for their livelihood.*

The Lore Lindu National Park in Central Sulawesi covers a range of habitats. The greater part of the park is over 1,000 metres (3,300 feet) above sea level and, owing to the low rainfall it receives, has large expanses of grass plains (above). Higher up, the plains give way to montane forest in which flowers such as (left) this Impatiens, *more familiarly known as the Busy Lizzie, can be found. Megalithic standing stones are a feature of the park.*

The forests of Indonesia are host to literally thousands of different species of orchid. Most are epiphytic – growing on other plants – but some grow on the forest floor. Two colourful examples are (above left and top right) Vanda hastifera and Spathoglottis plicata blume.

Right: Rhododendron javanicum var. schadenbergii is found near volcanic craters in Sulawesi and the Philippines.

Far right above and below: Pitcher plants like the Nepenthes maximus supplement the little natural nutrient available to them under the forest canopy by trapping small insects in a rolled leaf tip filled with liquid containing digestive enzymes.

Above left: *A sandy cove on Batudaka Island, one of the Togian Islands off Central Sulawesi.*

Above: *Coconut palms frame a view of the Tangkoko-Batuangus Nature Reserve in North Sulawesi. The lowland rainforest in this small reserve is home to many of Sulawesi's endemic species.*

Left: *Wooden ploughs and buffalo are traditionally used in irrigated paddy fields. Where the fields are very small, preparing the soil may even be done by hand. White egrets follow the plough on the look-out for small fish, frogs and other aquatic creatures.*

Opposite: *A view across to Manado Bay, near the capital of North Sulawesi. Here, on Sulawesi's snaking northern peninsula, is the beautiful Minahasa region with its volcanoes, lakes and white sand beaches.*

Above: *The Banda Islands were the centre for the production of mace and nutmeg, and their location was a closely guarded secret until their discovery by the Portuguese in 1511. The Portuguese, the English and the Dutch fought for their control from then on. Deserted forts and dilapidated Dutch villas bear testimony to this struggle. Mount Api Island is an active volcano in the centre of the group. The path of volcanic ash and lava from its last eruption, in 1988, can be clearly seen to the right of this picture, with a small, green oasis of a village at the water's edge.*

Opposite: *The island groups of Kei and Aru are uplifted coral reefs in the far east of Indonesia, near the south-western tip of Irian Jaya. Kei Kecil (above) is heavily forested and supports many rare species. The surrounding waters are full of fish, turtles and the only herbivorous marine mammal, the Dugong (Dugong dugon). The people of these islands are great boatbuilders, and decorate their boats with woodcarving and shells.*

An enduring and powerful sultanate existed on the island of Ternate (above), founded on the production of cloves. It was one of the first places in Maluku to have a permanent Portuguese and Dutch presence, and the ruins of old fortifications abound. In the centre of the island is the active volcano, Mount Gamalama (left).

The island of Hiri (above) lies to the north of Ternate. Ternate and Tidore, its neighbouring island, though separated by only a few kilometres, were ruled by different sultanates. They vied with each other for control of the spice trade and tended to throw in their lots with different European invaders. Each island is dominated by a volcano: the slopes of Mount Kiematubu on Tidore are thickly forested (right).

Irian Jaya is the Indonesian half of the island of New Guinea. The Dutch deliberately established their colonial capital, Hollandia, close to the border with German New Guinea (now Papua New Guinea) to underline their possession of the western half of the island. The town is now Jayapura, Irian's administrative centre and gateway to the interior. The bay (above) on which it is situated faces the vast sweep of the Pacific Ocean. Nearby is the Cyclops Mountain Reserve (left), an isolated range of steep hills whose varied habitats shelter some rare species.

Irian Jaya has a number of permanently snow-capped mountains and this glacier (above) along the line of the equator at Puncak Jaya in the Sudirman Mountains is at an altitude of 5,039 metres (16,532 feet). The glacier is now retreating quite rapidly, and is currently of great interest worldwide in terms of global warming.

Right: This unusual two-toned rhododendron (Rhododendron zoelleri), here growing at about 2,000 metres (6,600 feet) in Irian Jaya, is found from Seram to New Guinea.

Far right: Doreri Bay near Manokwari in north-western Irian Jaya.

The great swamp forests of southern Irian Jaya are crossed by large, slow-moving rivers such as the meandering Timika River (above) near Amamapare. Primitive cycads grow in the swamplands, such as the Cycas circinalis found in the Wasur-Rawa Biru National Park (left). They are related to an extinct group of plants, the seed-ferns, which flourished some 200 million years ago.

The Baliem Valley in Irian Jaya (above) was totally
isolated from the rest of the world until it was
discovered by mining surveyors in 1938. The valley is
at an altitude of some 1,500 metres (5,000 feet) and
its flat floor has given rise to a sophisticated
drainage and irrigation system for growing
vegetables. A typical village of the Dani people who
live in the valley (right) has the traditional domed huts
and enclosed vegetable beds.

THE PEOPLE

T he first people to inhabit Indonesia probably arrived some 30,000 years
ago, crossing the land bridges that then linked the islands to the main
Asian landmass. Although modern Indonesians are descendants of much
later Mongoloid migrations from southern China, traits of the earlier Australoid
peoples can still be detected in the ethnic groups of Irian Jaya and elsewhere.

Maritime trade throughout the Indonesian archipelago brought with it an
influx of peoples from the Middle East, from India and from the modern
civilizations of South-east Asia. The indigenous cultures were pushed back
gradually into the interior of the islands and the peoples of the coastal regions
became blended into a great diversity of racial types.

Indonesian society today is based largely on agriculture. Rice is the staple food
of the country and is grown at many levels of sophistication from the highly
organized irrigated paddy fields of Java and Bali to the slash-and-burn shifting
cultivation of dry rice in many other areas. In the eastern islands, where rice is
harder to grow, traditional crops include sago, sweet potato and coconut.
Marvellous fruits grow in the tropical climate and a huge variety of other plants
provide the basic materials for housing, clothes and the necessities of everyday life.

While most of Indonesia's population is rural, great cities have grown along the
trade routes from India and the Middle East to China and from the spice islands
of eastern Indonesia in the opposite direction. Modern industries have developed
from the plantations of the 19th century and Indonesia remains the major world
producer of rubber and palm oil. Oil and gas are major exports. Tin, copper, gold
and silver are all found in large quantities. Heavy industry thrives in steel and
cement works and aircraft production. Tourism is a rapidly expanding foreign
exchange earner and holidaymakers are flooding in from all over the world.

PREVIOUS PAGES
Page 94. Above left: *Rejang classical dance at a temple in Bali. The dancer wears the formal* kemben, *a band of cloth wound around the body leaving the shoulders bare.*
Above right: *Muslim Batak children on Samosir Island, North Sumatra.*
Below left: *A Dani farmer and his sons in the Baliem Valley, Irian Jaya.*
Below right: *Woman in traditional dress in Yogyakarta, Central Java.*
Page 95: *Fishing boats under sail off the coast of Madura in East Java.*

Above: *Villagers near Padang Sidenpuan in West Sumatra use the river running past their homes for bathing and washing clothes.*

Below right: *A Sumatran tribesman in traditional dress.*

OPPOSITE PAGE
Above: *The front of a typical Batak house on Samosir Island in North Sumatra. The massive saddleback roof covers a dark interior living space occupied by several families. The space under the main structure houses domestic animals.*

Below left: *Water buffalo are used to pull the ploughs in paddy fields near Bukittinggi in West Sumatra.*

Below right: *This magnificent royal house near Paya Kumbuh in West Sumatra is an opulent example of traditional Minangkabau architecture, with the extravagantly upswept gable ends of its huge roof.*

The traditional architecture of Toraja villages shares the saddleback roofs seen in Sumatra (top). The buffalo horns (above) demonstrate the power and wealth of the owner of this house.

Left: *Toraja farmers dry their rice in heaps on the ground, and make small 'haystacks' of the stalks.*

102

Above: *The bullock cart, whose wheels have been salvaged from some pre-war Mercedes Benz truck, is a common and efficient way of transporting rice for sale at the local market on to the government rice authority,* BULOG.

Right: *This Kanum hunter on the coastal plain of south-east Irian Jaya is out for whatever he can get, be it Bustard, Cassowary or Wallaby.*

FOLLOWING PAGES: *Siatu Kampung, a waterside village in the Togian Islands of Central Sulawesi.*

The export of copra, the dried kernel of the coconut, is an important part of the economy of Indonesia. The oil yielded by copra is used in food products and in the manufacture of cosmetics, soap and synthetic materials. This man in northern Maluku (above) is splitting coconuts to extract the kernel, watched by his wife and children. Coconut collectors like this one in West Sumatra (left) train Pig-tailed Macaques (Macaca nemestrina) to climb the coconut palms, pick the ripe nuts and throw them down. The collector will take a percentage of the plantation owner's crop to sell as his fee for the job.

On many small plantations in Indonesia, which do not have the central facilities of the large commercial concerns, local processing methods are used. In Sumatra, ripe coffee beans (above) are put out to dry on the main road, where the passage of carts and vehicles will shatter the husks. Cocoa pods (right) are spliced open by hand on a plantation in East Java.

Tea was introduced to Indonesia from China via India and is now a substantial plantation crop in highland regions. The leaf tips are harvested by hand (above) and then graded and dried in a central factory. Another important plantation crop is rubber. The latex is collected in cups which would once have been a half coconut shell but are now more often plastic (far left). The Oil Palm was brought to Indonesia as an ornamental plant in 1848 and exploited for its oil only at the beginning of the 20th century. The fresh fruit bunches (left) are sterilized and crushed to produce an edible oil which is also valuable in some industrial processes.

Cloves, nutmeg and mace were some of the spices over which the European powers went to war. For centuries the Banda Islands in Maluku were the only source of nutmeg and mace and the tiny island of Ternate in North Maluku the sole source of cloves. Cloves are generally grown in small plantations (above). The spice is the flower bud, which is picked just before it opens and then dried. The Nutmeg tree produces a fruit containing a single large seed (the nutmeg) with a bright red covering (mace). Both are spread out to dry in the sun (right).

The markets of Indonesia are its life-blood. People shop daily for food in a country with little refrigeration and a hot climate. In addition to the established markets, all the roads out of the main cities sprout roadside stalls selling seasonal fruit (above left), in this case rambutans. In Kalimantan, where roads are few and far between, farmers bring their produce by boat to a floating market, as at Banjarmasin (left). In the few areas where cattle are raised, such as West Sumatra, cattle markets (below left) are usually held outdoors. The Indonesian love of caged birds – nearly all caught in the wild – has brought some species close to extinction. Although the trade is now more closely controlled, bird markets (below) are common and are still a threat to wild birds.

Opposite: Town markets like these in North Sulawesi (above) and Yogyakarta (below left) display a huge range of fruit and vegetables. Some stalls may have more exotic fare to offer, such as barbecued rats. The food of Padang in West Sumatra (below right) is found in Padang restaurants all over Indonesia. A selection of hot, spicy dishes is placed on the table and you pay only for what you eat.

Fishing platforms (above) *are common in the shallow waters off the south-east coast of Sumatra. They serve as a place to dry nets and a seasonal dwelling for the fishermen. Off the Java coast the water deepens and the fishermen use boats operating out of small riverine ports* (left).

Opposite: *The seafaring Bugis people originated in southern Sulawesi and set out from Ujung Pandang (formerly Makassar) in their elegant schooners to become legendary traders throughout the Indonesian archipelago. Though many of their beautiful boats are now fitted with engines, they are still hand-built with traditional tools and without plans.*

Outrigger canoes of very similar design are the traditional small craft of Bali (above) *and Lombok* (right). *They are still used for fishing and, perhaps more lucratively, now serve to give pleasure trips to tourists.*

Opposite: *Javanese fishing boats and river ferries near Cirebon on the north coast of Java* (above). *Fish, both fresh and dried, is a vital part of the Indonesian diet. These wading fishermen in Central Sulawesi* (below left) *are catching milk fish larvae which will be sent to stock fish farms in Java. Below right: A boy in the Togian Islands, Central Sulawesi, with a load of fish on their way to be dried.*

The movement of people from over-populated Java to the outer islands has resulted in extensive clearing of rainforest for use as agricultural land, as here in Central Sulawesi (above). Elsewhere the land is scarred by mineral workings. Small gold mines such as this one near Cempaka in Central Kalimantan (left) and the diamond mines in the same area are often family affairs for reasons of security.

Above: *The vast mineral reserves of Irian Jaya are only now being exploited. The Freeport copper mine is situated at 3,700 metres (12,000 feet) in the Sudirman range.*

Right: *On Mount Ijen in East Java, sulphur is collected from the crater lake by more traditional means, carried in baskets over the crater rim and down the mountain.*

Left: *Lake Maninjau, about 50 km (30 miles) from Bukittinggi in West Sumatra, is a beautiful crater lake with lovely views. A small mosque nestles among the palms by the lake edge.*

Below: *A traditional Sundanese wedding in West Java.*

OPPOSITE PAGE:

Above: *A boat-shaped Batak tomb on Samosir Island in Lake Toba, North Sumatra. Though the Batak are now generally Christian or Muslim, they retain many of their animist traditions.*

Below left: *Muslim school girls.*

Below right: *Making offerings at a Chinese temple in Jakarta.*

The great Mahayana Buddhist monument of Borobudur in Central Java (top) is a portrait in stone of the cosmic world and a representation of the sacred mountain inhabited by the gods. It was built around AD 800 and the subjects of its carvings rise from the cares and passions of everyday life at the base to the topmost stupa representing Nirvana, eternal nothingness (left). The lower terraces are covered with lively bas-reliefs of daily and courtly life in 9th-century Java and scenes from the life of the Buddha (above centre), as well as animals and birds (above).

When the courts of Central Java changed their faith from Buddhism to Hinduism, the great temple of Borobudur was abandoned soon after its completion and work started in the latter part of the 9th century on a Hindu monument. Prambanan (top) is a complex of eight candi on a raised terrace, of which the largest (left) is dedicated to Shiva. To the north-west of Borobudur and Prambanan is the Dieng Plateau, site of some of the oldest Hindu temples in Java (above).

Opposite: Pura Besakih, the Mother Temple of Bali, is the largest on the island and every district has its own temple or shrine in it. It was built some ten centuries ago on terraces about 1,000 metres (3,300 feet) up the slopes of the sacred Mount Agung.

With the coming of Islam, Hinduism was extinguished on Java and developed on Bali in isolation. It remains the most pervasive force in Balinese life, with almost no distinction between the secular and the religious: every part of daily life is regulated or influenced by it. Votive offerings (left) are carried to the village temple by families everywhere. There are many temples built on a grander scale (below left), among which is the Ulu Danu Water Temple on Lake Bratan in the mountainous centre of Bali (bottom left). Cremations are of great significance on Bali and the funeral pyre is richly ornamental with offerings and mystic beasts such as this lion (below).

Of all Bali's temples, Tanah Lot (below) *is probably the most visited and photographed. Its spectacular setting on a rocky outcrop offshore makes it irresistible to every photographer, particularly at sunset.*

A cremation (right) *and a religious procession along the tourist beach at Kuta* (bottom) *show how the religious life of Bali continues alongside the all-pervasive tourism.*

Like the Balinese, the Toraja people of Central Sulawesi conduct their funerals in two parts. The first is a simple affair immediately following death. The second, a ceremony of great pomp, must be delayed until the arrangements have been made, sufficient funds raised and the presence of relations and friends assured. The funeral ceremony of an important village headman takes place outside the village but mourners first gather under the great roofs of their traditional Toraja houses (above) to sing dirges before the funeral bier (left) is carried out to the funeral ground.

The Toraja dead are buried in various ways but the wealthy commission burial caves in neighbouring cliffs. The entrance opening may be small but the internal chamber can accommodate whole families (above). Effigies of the dead are placed as if on a balcony outside the cave entrances. These tau tau are now carved with some attempt at realism: the statue of a revered relative (right) smokes his favourite pipe, surrounded by his smiling family. The Toraja consider the ceremonial funeral a happy event as it speeds the dead person to the afterworld where he will not bring misfortune on his earthly family, as might be the case if the rites were not correctly observed.

The courts of Central Java achieved their present form in the late 18th century, when the Kraton, or palaces, of Yogyakarta and Surakarta were built. Top: The Reception Hall of the Kraton of Surakarta (more usually known as Solo). *Much of the decoration is formal Javanese (above) but many European additions were made in the 1920s and 1930s. Court ritual is still strictly observed, such as the formal daily preparation of tea for the sultan in Yogyakarta (left).*

In Yogyakarta the sultan's palace is home to possibly thousands of courtiers (above) *many of whom are 'grace and favour' residents or members of the sultan's extended family. The style of headdress once indicated the status of the wearer and certain batik patterns were reserved for the sultan's close relatives. The Prophet Mohammed's birthday is marked by a major festival, the Sekatan. These men* (bottom) *have been taking part in the procession.*

The Kraton of Yogya and Solo have numerous gamelan orchestras which are used for different occasions. At the Sekatan festival in Yogya, the ancient gamelan (below) is brought out from the Kraton mosque and carried to the Great Mosque. Other gamelan played by court musicians accompany dances in the pavilions of the Kraton (left) .

Right
ancie
in the
elsew
waya

Belc
read
the
rule
enth

Abov

Right
youn
Legc
teen:
of th
dres
of ea

The gamelan, *found in both Java and Bali, is an almost entirely percussive orchestra, consisting of metallophones, gongs and a two-stringed fiddle. The ensembles of the two regions are superficially similar but differences in tuning and the way they are played give the Balinese instruments* (above) *a brighter and lighter sound than the Javanese* gamelan *such as this one* (right) *being played on the north coast of Java. The metallophones and smaller gongs are mounted on supports which are sometimes intricately carved and gilded. The* gamelan *is the essential accompaniment for* wayang kulit *or shadow-puppet plays, celebrations and dances in the royal Kraton of Java and the temples of Bali.*

Although the men of the Dani tribe live in the Baliem Valley in Irian Jaya at an altitude of over 1,500 metres (5,000 feet) above sea level, they wear no warm clothing (above). Their traditional costume consists largely of headdresses and extravagantly proportioned penis sheaths. The Dayaks of Kalimantan wear grass coats and brilliantly coloured masks (left) in a ritual dance to drive away bad spirits. The performers' movements are inspired by the flight of the hornbill.

Opposite: Children on the island of Kei Kecil in North Maluku perform a dance called 'The Welcome to the Returning Warrior' on the beach.

Ce...
go...
m...
la...
m...
m...

A...

Klungkung in Bali is still a centre of traditional painting and crafts, as illustrated by the painted ceiling of the Hall of Justice (left). In the 1930s a new form of painting developed with the encouragement of two European artists resident in Bali (lower left). Following a period of stagnation during and after the Second World War, two other resident European painters encouraged the development of the so-called 'Young Artists' group in Ubud in the 1960s (below). Brighter and more exuberant than before, it commonly portrays themes of present-day village life in Bali.

Beadwork and other decorative forms are much used by the Dayaks of Kalimantan. The broad hat and decorated baby basket (right) *are typical of the patterns used in the Mahakam River area. The ceremonial headdress* (below left) *is worn by a Kayan man from the same district. Beadwork is commonly worn by women in Central Sulawesi such as this headband* (below right) *on a Lore woman.*

Batik is the art of decorating cloth by the resist method using repeated applications of wax on the material before each dying (top). In batik tulis the wax is applied with a small funnelled cup (left). In the later form, batik cap, *a patterned block of copper strips is used (above).*

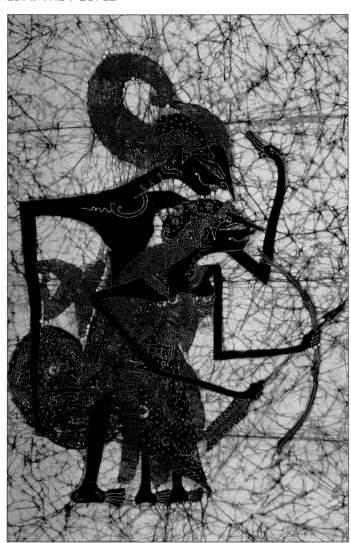

Batik comes in all forms. The Javanese tradition employs over 3,000 patterns. Modern designs may be stylized (above) or employ traditional Javanese images such as these wayang kulit *figures (above right). Modern designs using bright colours in non-traditional compositions are also common. This modern batik (right) is by the artist Agus Darmaji of Yogyakarta.*

Opposite: *Weaving, though it employs very ancient techniques, is still a vibrant craft in many parts of Indonesia, particularly in North Sumatra where Batak cloth such as the* kain kulos *blanket being made on a hand loom (above) is much prized. Other areas famous for their weaving skills are Kalimantan and Nusa Tenggara, where this woman is spinning thread (below right). Double* ikat *weaving demands a high level of skill. The weavers of the village of Tenganan in Bali are famous for this technique (below left).*

This page: *Some examples of traditional patterns from Sulawesi (above); the Batak people of North Sumatra (above right); a Toraja pattern from Central Sulawesi (right) and from the Balinese village of Tenganan (below right).*

THE WILDLIFE

The astonishing diversity of wildlife in Indonesia is due in part to the rich natural environment which varies from dense tropical rainforest and swamp to snow-capped mountains and dry savannahs. With only about one per cent of the world's land surface, Indonesia supports 10 per cent of its plant species, 12 per cent of its mammals, 16 per cent of its reptiles and 17 per cent of its birds. The eastern part of the country was once linked to Australia and it retains typical Australian forms of life, such as kangaroos and parrots. The west was once linked to the Asian mainland, and large Asian land animals such as elephants, rhinoceros, tigers and leopards are still found in Sumatra and Borneo.

Many of the plant and animal species of the rainforest have not yet even been identified, and many are endemic to Indonesia. Among animal superlatives are the Komodo Dragon, the world's largest lizard; the Reticulated Python, the world's largest snake; the *Rafflesia*, the largest flower and *Chalocodoma pluto*, the world's largest bee.

The archipelago of Indonesia is mostly sea: a sea which is often completely clean and unpolluted. Gorgeous coral reefs abound, in and around which glide brilliantly coloured tropical fish. Sea turtles return every year to the same beaches to lay their eggs.

In an attempt to limit the destruction caused to the environment by indiscriminate exploitation of the forests and seas, the Indonesian government has set up a number of nature reserves in various parts of the country. Within these parks, ecotourism is encouraged and the income thus generated is used to offset the costs of maintaining the parks and continuing the scientific research carried out in them.

Above: *The long sandy beaches of the Meru Betiri National Park in East Java are favoured by Green Turtles (Chelonia mydas)* for laying their eggs. The eggs are protected by the park management.

Left: *A shoal of small fishes swim around a soft coral (Dendronephthya) off the island of Flores.*

PREVIOUS PAGES
Page 146. Above left: *A young Orang-utan (Pongo pygmaeus) in Central Kalimantan.*
Above right: *A gorgonian sea fan with a number of crinoids, or featherstars, in its branches.*
An Eclectus parrot (below left) *and* (below right) *the Spotted Cuscus (Spilocuscus maculatus) are examples of Australian-derived wildlife in Irian Jaya.*
Page 147: *The Crested Lizard (Calotes cristatellus) is a common visitor to gardens in Kalimantan.*

Nusa Tenggara and Maluku in eastern Indonesia have some of the clearest sea-water and most brilliantly coloured corals and fish to be found anywhere. The waters around the island of Flores are particularly rich and easy of access.

Right: *A pink Anemone Fish* (Amphiprion perideraion) *at home in its sea anemone,* Heteractis magnifica. *Many small reef fish shelter from predators by nestling within the waving tentacles of an anemone. A substance in their body mucus, acquired from the anemone itself, protects them from the stinging cells of their host.*

Below: *A Zebra Lionfish* (Dendrochirus brachypterus). *Its spines carry a powerful poison and a sting from an adult lionfish causes severe pain.*

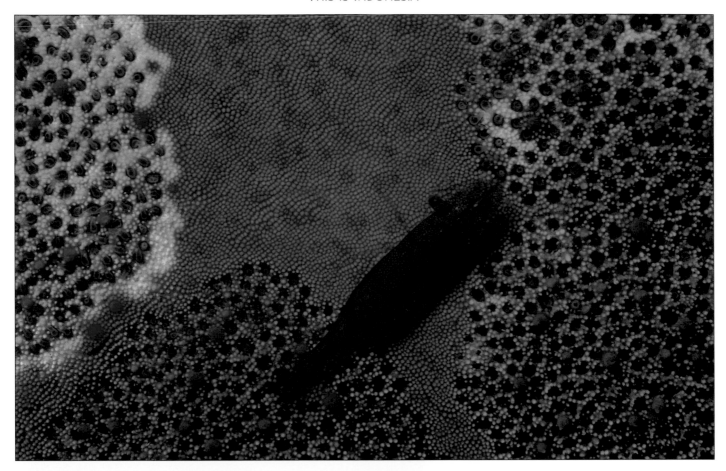

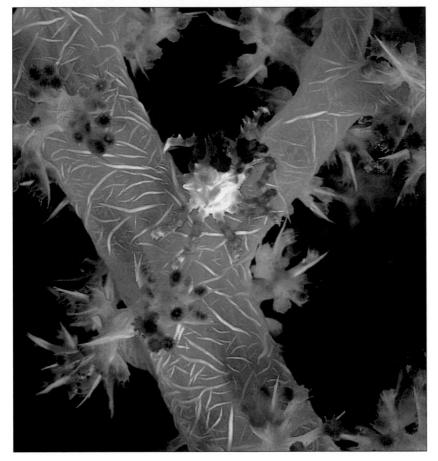

Above: *A shrimp* (Periclemenes soror) *feeding on a Pin-cushion Starfish* (Culcita novaeguinae). *Various, often colourful, species of shrimp inhabit a reef, usually living in association with corals, anemones and sea stars.*

Left: *A spider crab* (Hoplophrys) *on soft coral* (Dendronephthya). *Some spider crabs provide themselves with protective camouflage by carrying pieces of sponge or coral on their backs.*

Opposite: *The featherstar, a crinoid, is distantly related to starfish and sea urchins. Unlike them, it spends part of its life attached by a stalk to a rock in the shallows, feeding on micro-organisms that drift past. However, the adult featherstar is also able to swim freely.*

*The brilliant diversity of the coral reefs off the island of Flores in
Nusa Tenggara can be seen here, as a shoal of basslets
(Pseudanthias) and other brightly coloured fish swim over the coral.
Small fish often swim together in mixed shoals to gain greater
protection from predators.*

Top: *A candy-striped sea cucumber* (Thelenota). *The ring of tentacles surrounding the mouth is used to sweep up organic matter.*

Above: *A female Green Turtle* (Chelonia mydas) *returns to the sea after laying her eggs on Sukamade Beach in the Meru Betiri National Park in East Java.*

Indonesia is the home of many reptiles, including (left) the Flying Lizard (Draco volans) and (above) the large Monitor Lizard (Varanus salvator) which can grow to a length of 2.5 metres (8 feet). Crocodiles are farmed commercially in many parts of South-east Asia. The skins of these crocodiles in a farm near Jayapura in Irian Jaya (below) will end up as expensive shoes and handbags.

Rinca Island (right) *in the Komodo National Park is famous as the home of the Komodo Dragon* (Varanus komodoensis), *the heaviest lizard in the world. These monsters* (below left) *can grow to a length of 3 metres (10 feet) and weigh up to 50 kilograms (110 pounds). They are common in the Komodo National Park and on the west coast of the nearby island of Flores, but are found nowhere else. However, they are not a survival of the age of dinosaurs but a modern, evolving lizard. These six-week old babies* (below right) *were the first to be born in captivity in Jakarta Zoo.*

Sumatran Elephants (Elephas maximus), *such as these two bathing in the Way Kambas National Park in Sumatra (top), are both a protected species and a local pest, able to destroy large areas of plantations.* Left: The Sumatran Rhinoceros (Dicerorhinus sumatrensis) *has a viable future probably only in Sumatra, though small populations are found elsewhere in South-east Asia. Another rare species (above)* is the Babirusa (Babyrousa babyrussa), *found only in Sulawesi. The extraordinary curving tusks of the male pierce its cheeks; this characteristic is found in no other living creature.*

Top and right: *The Timor Deer* (Cervus timorensis), *an ancient introduction into Irian Jaya and Sulawesi, is now relatively common.*

Above: *Although a protected species, the Sambar Deer* (Cervus unicolor) *is often illegally hunted. It is still relatively common in western Indonesia.*

The insect species of Indonesia far outnumber all its other fauna. Grasshoppers (above left) present a serious threat to young rice plants, as a swarm can quickly eat the young leaves of a whole crop. Brightly coloured Hemipteran bugs (top) suck sap from leaves. Other forest dwellers include (left) bush crickets (Tettigonidae), and (above) beetles such as the leaf-eating Jewel Beetle (Chrysochroa fulminans).

Opposite: *Many spectacular butterflies grace the forests of Indonesia:* (above) *Five-bar Swallowtail* (Graphium antiphates itamputi); (below left) *Bluebottle;* (below right) *Glorious Begum* (Agatasa caledonia), *Nawab* (Polyura *species*), *Sergeant* (Athyma *species*) *and Blue Nawab* (Polyura schreiber) *feeding together on the forest floor.*

Mount Leuser National Park in North Sumatra and Tanjung Puting National Park on the south coast of Kalimantan both have Orang-utan rehabilitation centres, where young Orang-utans rescued from agricultural forest clearance or captivity in city homes can be prepared for self-sufficiency in the wild. The Camp Leakey Research Station in Tanjung Puting has been made famous by Dr Biruté Galdikas, who has worked there for 20 years.

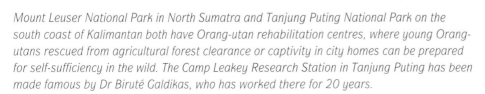

Baby Orang-utans (Pongo pygmaeus) *are considered status-symbol (if illegal) pets. If discovered and confiscated they are taken to a rehabilitation centre where they are initially fed regularly (above) but gradually encouraged to fend for themselves in the wild. This is a long process as the young apes would naturally have stayed with their mother for at least eight years, learning her survival techniques. Wild males (right) sometimes come to the rehabilitation centres to mate with semi-wild females.*

Left: *The Black Macaque* (Macaca nigra) *is one of a number of macaques found in Indonesia; there are many subspecies.*

Below left: *The Long-tailed Macaque* (Macaca fascicularis) *is the commonest Indonesian monkey, widespread from Sumatra to Lombok. It is tolerant of many different environments, including human settlements. It is equally catholic in its diet: it may collect leaves and fruit, or catch crabs and small animals. Where it has become accustomed to tourists and the food they carry, as in Bali, it can become an aggressive nuisance.*

Below: *Thomas' Leaf Monkey* (Presbytis thomasi) *is common in Aceh. It is a leaf-eater and possesses a stomach divided into separate sacs which allow the leaves to be broken down slowly into digestible compounds, functioning in much the same way as cows' stomachs.*

Gibbons, the smallest of the apes, are monogamous and live in family groups. They all sing loudly: a pair may perform a complicated duet or the male may sing by himself. The Siamang (Hylobates syndactylus) is the largest species (above). The Moloch, or Javan Gibbon (Hylobates moloch) is now found only in West and Central Java (below right). The Proboscis Monkey (Nasalis larvatus) is found only in Borneo. It is a strong swimmer and has partially webbed feet.

Below: One of the most attractive primates is the tiny nocturnal Spectral Tarsier (Tarsius spectrum), weighing only 100 grams (4 ounces).

Cuscus are marsupial tree bears found from North Australia to Sulawesi. Above: *The Spotted Cuscus (Spilocuscus maculatus) inhabits Irian Jaya, while (below) the Dwarf Cuscus (Strigocuscus celebensis) is found in Sulawesi together with the larger Bear Cuscus.*

Opposite: *This Tree-kangaroo (left and above right) is a recently discovered species called Dendrolagus mbaiso which was caught near Puncak Jaya. As it is revered as an ancestor by local tribes it is generally not hunted. The Dani tribesman holding the young animal was hoping to sell it. The Dani call it 'bondegezou', which means 'man of the alpine forest' in their language.*

Below right: *The Black Tree-kangaroo (Dendrolagus orsinus) is also endemic to Irian Jaya. Tree-kangaroos do not have the highly developed hind legs of the terrestrial species; instead they are provided with strong claws for gripping branches. They are much more at home in the trees than on the ground, where they appear ungainly. Most species are solitary and nocturnal, though some are sociable and move around during the day.*

Above: *Rinca Island in the Komodo National Park in Nusa Tenggara is home to a herd of about 300 horses descended from those introduced in the 19th century by the sultan of Bima for breeding. They are now completely wild.*

The Warty Hog (Sus verrucosus) *is endemic to Java, where it is often hunted for sport (left). Three pairs of warts on its face distinguish it from the common wild boar* (Sus scrofa), *seen opposite above with wild cattle* (Bos javanicus) *in the Ujung Kulon National Park in Java.*

Opposite, below left: *Two Agile Wallabies* (Wallabia agilis) *in south-east Irian Jaya show their highly developed hind legs.*

Below right: *The Short-beaked Echidna, or Spiny Anteater* (Tachyglossus aculeatus). *Echidnas are egg-layers like the Australian Platypus.*

Above: *Purple Herons* (Ardea purpurea) *at a heronry in Jakarta Bay.* Far left: *The Lesser Tree-duck* (Dendrocygna javanica) *and* (below left) *the Greater Adjutant Stork* (Leptoptilos dubius) *are widespread in South and South-east Asia, whereas the Masked Lapwing* (Vanellus miles) *is, in Indonesia, found only in Irian Jaya* (above left).

Opposite above: *Sheepmaker's Crowned Pigeon, one of three species of the genus Goura found only in Irian Jaya.*

Below left to right: *Blyth's Hornbill* (Rhyticeros plicatus) *is an Asian bird for which Irian Jaya is its eastern limit, whereas the Southern or Two-wattled Cassowary* (Casuarius casuarius) *and the Australian Pelican* (Pelecanus conspicillatus) *both arrived in Irian Jaya from Australia.*

Above left: *The Purple Moorhen (Porphyrio porphyrio) inhabits swampy areas throughout South-east Asia. Its huge feet enable it to walk easily over floating vegetation.*

Above right: *Green Jungle Fowl (Gallus varius) occur only in Java, Flores and Sumba.*

Left: *Male Lesser Bird of Paradise (Paradisaea minor). The feathers of the birds of paradise were known in Europe over 600 years ago, and have also long been prized by the inhabitants of Irian Jaya for their ceremonial regalia.*

Parrots, cockatoos and lorys all derive from Australia and are obvious signs that you have crossed to the east of Wallace's Line. Above: *The Black-capped Lory* (Lorius lory) *is found as far west as the Maluku and, below, the Rainbow Lorikeet* (Trichoglossus haematodus) *as far west as Bali.*

The Red-sided Eclectus Parrot (Eclectus roratus) *is one of the few parrots in which the sexes can easily be told apart: the female is red and blue and the male* (right) *is green.*

FOLLOWING PAGE
The fabulous display of the Javanese Peacock (Pavo muticus).

INDEX